ONE LOT AT A TIME

One Lot at a Time

ISBN (paperback): 978-1-963271-70-6
ISBN (Ebook): 978-1-963271-71-3

Armin Lear Press, Inc.
215 W Riverside Drive, #4362
Estes Park, CO 80517

ONE LOT AT A TIME

CREATING A LIFE OF WEALTH & FREEDOM
THROUGH LAND INVESTING

DANIEL APKE

ARMINLEAR

CONTENTS

INTRODUCTION

There is a glut of information available about real estate investing—countless websites, myriad podcasts, unending articles. The problem isn't a lack of information, it's finding a curated source of the *best* information. Real estate investing tends to attract a certain type of investor and businessperson. Let me throw a few words out here—entrepreneur, hard-working, goal-oriented, alternative thinker, a "work smarter not harder" philosophy. Sound familiar? Do you identify with those as much as I do? If you do, (and I think you do), then you are seeking a way to skip the trial and error, save time and money, and find the most efficient path to your goals. You're not alone. That was me several years ago, and it is who my students are. We have all experienced some sort of pain point in our lives that we want to reverse. Get rid of the crappy job. Make more money. Retire early. Be your own boss. It's cliché for a reason, but that doesn't make it any less true. And the absolute best way I've found to accomplish this (and I've tried more than a few) is by land investing.

Land investing and entrepreneurship changed my life. I went from making $65,000 working in Cincinnati, Ohio to making millions of dollars. You do not need a college education or any fancy background to make this work. Trust me . . . I had a 2.4 GPA in high school and didn't get into any colleges right out of high school. I promise you, if I can do it, anyone can. People often ask me why I got into this business. I have actually been involved in more than ten different business models over the years, and the reason I now focus on land investing is simple: it is the simplest, least competitive, and most profitable business I have seen.

The first couple chapters of this book will be about your journey and what to expect throughout the book. Then we will dive deep into the business of land investing. This is a how-to book that will take you from whatever stage you're currently at to being a knowledgeable land investor. I am going to share some of the mistakes I made on my journey to help you avoid those same mistakes and achieve what it is what you are looking for in life. I will guide you through everything you need to know about land investing to run a profitable, sustainable business.

When I founded Land Investing Online (LIO) it was not my objective to make more money. I had my land investing firm for that. It was and still is my mission to help others achieve the freedom they are looking for. This is simply the best way to do it. But this isn't a get rich quick scheme. There are no shortcuts, no easy money, no guarantees, and a certain amount of risk is still certainly involved. That's the reality of any business and any investment. Likewise, land investing requires dedication, hard work, and resilience, just like any other business. But your life will never change if you don't take action, and there is no better time than now.

WHAT IS FREEDOM?

What Is Freedom?

Freedom is defined as "the state of being able to act without hindrance or restraint."[1] Most people are restrained by their jobs, financial situation, or some other aspect of life. They don't have the time and flexibility to do what they want. Answer this—why did you buy this book? What changes in your life do you want to make? For me, I wanted to choose my location, and I wanted financial freedom. I wanted to be able to travel wherever I wanted on my own time and not worry about bills or finances. Not having to stress or worry about rent or bills is an incredible freedom to have. For you, it could be as simple as wanting to save up for your kid's college education or build a second reliable stream of income, so you have more financial flexibility. Maybe you want to get out of

---

1   "Freedom: Oxford English Dictionary," accessed February 18, 2024, https://www.oed.com/search/dictionary/?scope=Entries&q=freedom.

your day job because you hate your manager and working for other people. Many of you will say, "I just want to make more money." But why? What are your goals for that money? What will your life look like once you have that money? Jesse Itzler, an entrepreneur and life coach, has new entrepreneurs do a simple exercise to help with this. He simply asks, "What would you do if you received a billion dollars today?" Think about that, and once you have a clear answer, you can formulate your purpose and mission.

I have found that there usually is more to it than just wanting to make more money. I see it frequently among the members of my Land Investing Online program. I remember one member specifically—he just wanted to make money so he could ski every day. That was his purpose and that's what drove him to be as successful as he was. He was obsessed with skiing and land investing gave him the freedom to pursue it full time while investing on the side. That's what you need to find for yourself. Once you find out your *why*, write it down and review it every single day so you don't lose track of your purpose for reading this book and making drastic changes, for the better, in your life.

Finding the Right People

Once you find your *why* and your purpose, the next step is to find the right people in your life to hold you accountable. This could be your friends, family, and other loved ones. Holding yourself accountable can go a long way. Tell them your goals, your plans, and your *why*. Times will get tough, and when they do, you will need these people around you to be supporting you and pushing you to move forward and prevent you from quitting.

My brother Mike started his land investing career a little over three months prior to me writing this book. Mike called me a few weeks ago and said he's getting ready to quit land investing. He explained how he could make hundreds of thousands of dollars as a software engineer and have a safe job, and that he'd already spent over $6,000 on this business without getting crazy results. However, I knew he'd at least had some success because I was financing one of the properties he bought, and our father was financing another three.

Once I collected all the facts and analyzed his situation, I realized he was at a breaking point. He hadn't seen results because he has a few properties posted for sale that hadn't sold yet. I also realized he would make over $25,000 of profit after his properties sold and he'd paid back his investors (a.k.a. our dad and me.) He was at a point where he saw his expenses, saw the lack of return, and his anxiety and pessimism took over showing only the negative. It was my job to be neutral and provide some help.

Mike wasn't calling me to tell me he was quitting. He was calling me for advice. As his brother, I knew his goals intimately and I also truly wanted the best for him. When you're looking for your supporters, make sure that they are people who love you unconditionally and want the best from you and for you. I carefully choose who I share things with because, the fact is, there will be some people who don't believe in you or are jealous of your passion and drive. I believe everyone will come to a breaking point at some point in their business. I have had *many* breaking points, and I'm sure there will be one during the process of this book. (There was!) If this is your first time starting a business, the breaking points can seem much worse than they actually are. That's why people quit business and fail at entrepreneurship. But land investing is a proven business model. If the members of my program and I can do it, I promise you that you can do it as well. Find your accountability partner like Mike and I have. I call Mike all the time for different advice and help. If you have a sibling, parent, wife, cousin, or best friend who comes to mind as your person, tell them your goals and what you're trying to accomplish. Tell them your *why*. But be forewarned—the sad truth is some people will try to shut your goals and dreams down and tell you they're impossible. This book is a means to show you what's possible, and you can see the success stories of hundreds of other land investors' stories at Landinvestingonline.com/testimonials. Surround yourself with believers, not people who want to bring you down.

Envision Your Life

What do you see in your future? What matters most to you? Focus on them. Affirm in your mind, on paper, and out loud your ability to achieve them. By shaping your thoughts and vision, you'll shape your attitude which leads to stronger actions. With sound actions, success is inevitable. Think about what your life will look like once you accomplish your goals and have the freedom you are seeking. For me, my *why*, my goals, and my support team all enabled me to pay off debt, buy rental properties, travel the world, and spend more time with friends and family. I also bought a few other gadgets like a new car, a pool, sauna, ice bath, and other things I love while I was at it. Write down the three things you are going to do as soon as you achieve your freedom and review them every single day.

Here are some examples of goals from some of our members at Land Investing Online.

- Buy a bigger house for my family
- Have the ability to work and stay at home to raise children instead of putting them in daycare.
- Buy a vacation home
- Spend more time on hobbies like golfing and fishing
- Travel
- Pay off debt
- Increase savings for children's college education
- And many, many more . . .

If you need to list more than three goals, that is completely okay, but just make sure it's not so many that you lose focus. Three has been shown to be the perfect amount for most people to remember and reiterate every day. Over time, your thoughts will become your reality as long as you are continuing to take action. Consistency is key; you'll be surprised how one hour a day can change your life if you review and envision your goals consistently. You'll look back six months down the road and see how far you've come.

Another strategy I have seen work is vision boards. With so much going on in our everyday lives, we can easily lose track of our goals and vision. One goal review technique that is effective in business and personal development programs is vision boards. They are very simple. You gather pictures from the internet, magazines, or anywhere else and create a collage of the pictures on a corkboard or something similar. This technique is powerful because it quickly reminds you of your goals and vision. It reminds you of what the life you want looks like. For example, if you want to have more savings in your bank account, take a screenshot of your online banking portal, edit the numbers, and make it look like $526,582 instead of $5,265. Print that out and put them on your vision board. Print that out and put it on your vision board. If you want to travel more and buy a boat, print out a beautiful picture of the Ritz Carlton Resort and a picture of your dream boat, and add them to the collage.

There are probably a hundred other ways to envision your goals. Find what works for you and focus on it. Remember—consistency is key.

Four Levels of Why

In his book *Your Next Five Moves* Patrick Bet-David talks about your "Four Levels of Why."[2] The levels of why are ultimately stages that you pass through in life. These levels of why are in chronological order, so level four is the most desirable and level one is the least desirable. The sad part is most people never make it to their level three or four. Your goal is to find out where you are in these stages and make moves to enhance your future. The great Stoic philosopher Zeno said, "Well-being is realized by small steps, but truly no small thing." You're not going to make quantum leaps overnight. Instead, as you take consistent small steps and get small wins, you'll look back in the very near future and see how far you've come. It's okay to be in stage one of the four levels of why. The majority of us have been there, including myself. But once you put a plan in place and start attacking these small wins, you'll advance your well-being in no time.

---

2 Patrick Bet-David and Greg Dinkin, *Your Next Five Moves: Master the Art of Business Strategy* (New York City, NY: Gallery Books, 2020).

Level One: Survival

Level one is when you are stuck in a nine-to-five job, living pay-check to paycheck, and just working to pay off your bills. Almost everyone has been here at some point in their life, but many people stop here. The good news is that your goals, your vision, and reading this book will lead you out of this survival level and advance your future.

Level Two: Status

You'll hear people saying, "I want to make six figures." Why is that? Status. They may want to send their kids to prestigious schools, buy a nice house and buy cars. While I am a believer in buying and enjoying nice things if you have the means to, it is a different story when people buy them merely to brag about them or show them off. People who do this are not happy. Not really. It's at best a shallow type of happiness. Believe it or not, a janitor making $45,000 a year with true purpose will be much happier than an executive who makes $1,000,000 but who lacks purpose and buys things merely to prove he is financially free. When most people reach this status level, they slow down and settle. It can be very hard for people to make a move to another career or job when they have all these things. That's why finding your "why," or your purpose, is so important to moving on to level three.

Level Three: Freedom

Level three is having freedom. People may say, I'm sick and tired of making six figures. I want to be free and make the kind of money that gives me breathing room and not having to be in the office everyday reporting to my boss. Maybe you want to be a digital nomad traveling the world or live in a place where your kids can run around outside and be safe, or live in both Colorado and Florida, skiing in the winter and surfing in the summer. Freedom can be a huge step up from the previous two levels. It also can give you room to breathe and discover some of your other passions and projects. Level three acts as a steppingstone, and it's hard to get from level two to level four without stopping at level three first. For me, level three helped me attain freedom through my first drop-shipping store that was making millions every year. I saw how much this freedom did for me which motivated me to start Land Investing Online. I wanted to share my knowledge with my previous self—in other words, our members and you, the reader of this book.

Level Four: Purpose

Defining purpose is easy: How do you want to be remembered? How do you want to make an impact in other people's lives? It's about realizing why you were put on this earth and pushing the limits of the greatest version of yourself, your true potential. Unfortunately, very few people reach level four level because of fear. In reality, fear is what stops most people from doing most things, resulting in spending their entire lives stuck in the level one survival mode.

A member of my local community, Max, had a what appeared to be phenomenal job as a software developer for a startup in Washington. Max saved up money, enjoyed his freedom, and pursued land investing full time while enjoying much more time with his family. Being able to spend quality time with his family was his *why* and fulfilled him completely. He was able to make great money from land investing and spend more time as a stay-at-home father with his young kids. His *why* and his purpose came together.

Envision what your life will look like. Maybe you already know your purpose and maybe you do not. Either way that is okay and it will come with the freedom and experience you get from achieving your level three. I had no idea what I wanted to do but I knew I needed the freedom to find out.

Identifying Where You Are

Now that you have learned about the four stages of *why*, we must identify where you are in the process. As I mentioned, these stages are not permanent and can change with time and consistency. Be honest with yourself. Sometimes the hardest thing to do in life is to look in the mirror and reflect. Many of you are in stage one, survival mode, or stage two, status. To determine where you are in the process, ask yourself: Are you truly fulfilled at the end of each day? Do you feel drained after work? Does thinking of work add energy to you or drain your battery? Are you just working to pay your bills and feed your family?

Once you have identified where you are, we can now put metrics and goals in place to help move you forward. Keep reading this book and I will walk you through the strategies that have worked for myself and our members at Land Investing Online. These processes have taken years and years to develop and tweak.

Your Unique Journey

What is it in life you're looking to change? What attracted you to this book and topic? For many of you, it's probably dissatisfaction with your nine-to-five job. You're probably either looking to get out of your job or make more money to achieve the desired freedom you are looking for. In this section, we are going to discuss the journey and processes for entrepreneurs looking to make these changes. You have the ability to replace your nine-to-five job, make tons of money, and take a side hustle to a full-blown 1-percenter income with the flexibility and freedom that brings. After that, you will have the ability to quit your job or make serious changes in your life for the better.

Throughout this chapter, continue to focus on your purpose and what brought you here. You need to raise your standards in order to achieve these goals. Starting your day at 8:00 a.m. and clocking out at 5:00 p.m. may not cut it anymore. Work needs to be done, extra work, late work, seven days a week work, and there will be sacrifices. It comes down to your work, consistency, and execution. Follow the path of success that I've seen from successful mentees of mine and also learn from what I have experienced in my own life.

Nine-to-Five Job

Are you currently locked into a nine-to-five job? Is your nine-to-five job not fulfilling and not where you want to be? Do you have bigger dreams and aspirations than your current job? This is the case for most people reading this book. I had a nine-to-five job that I enjoyed. I just had bigger goals and dreams that I needed to pursue. By the time I quit my job, I had multiple other streams of income and was earning over five times what I earned at my nine-to-five job. That job was essential at first because it was a means to pay my bills and live my life in the survival phase.

Our most successful entrepreneurs keep their job until it is

safe for them to quit and move on. Keeping that job is also important because it gives the entrepreneur resources to reinvest into the
business instead of paying a salary. Here's an example from one of
our members, Markus. Markus was making $10,000 a month with
his W2 job as an inside salesman. He started his side business as a
land investor and within six months he was making over $10,000
a month. Since he kept his inside sales job, Markus was able to
reinvest that $10,000 earned from his land investing company
into the business instead of paying himself a salary. He took that
profit and put it into marketing and buying more properties. That
investment quickly replicated. Within six months he was able to
earn over $50,000 a month. Once he was earning much more than
his income, he was able to quit his job, pay himself a great salary,
and still reinvest plenty of money.

It should be noted that quitting too early can be risky. Take
Lauren for example: she was working as a marketing assistant at
a Fortune 500 company making $5,000 a month. Lauren disliked
her corporate culture and was excited to quit and get out of there.
She started land investing and was making $5,000 a month. As
soon as she hit $5,000 a month, she could pay herself a salary and
quit her job, so she did. This gave her very little additional income
to reinvest into marketing and purchasing properties. She started
feeling desperate and "needed" this to work. She then became
scared to invest additional money in marketing because she was
worried she wouldn't have enough to pay herself a salary. Lauren
got through the tough times, but it took her about sixteen months
to make $50,000 a month.

Using your extra side hustle money for reinvestments is
crucial. Markus was able to make $50,000 in six months, while

Lauren took sixteen months to do the same. This is simply because one was reinvesting heavily and the other was reinvesting very timidly. Money compounds over time and putting your reinvestments into the right places early makes a huge difference, as you saw in this example. Make the sacrifices early by reinvesting into your business and it will pay tremendous dividends later.

If you don't currently want to leave your nine-to-five job, I'm sure there are other reasons you are at this level. If you love your job and just want to make more money, that is completely fine, and I respect that. You can do this as a part-time side hustle and even scale it. The only difference is you'll need to find the time outside your regular hours to get the work done. We have many members in our program who do this and there is absolutely nothing wrong with that.

Side Hustle

As we explained in the previous pages, most people must start their entrepreneurial journey as a side hustle. This is simply because it is not realistic to have this as a full time job right away. It takes time and consistency to build up to the point where you're making a full-time income. There will be sacrifices that need to be made to get this side-hustle off the ground and running. Some people like to wake up before their nine-to-five job. Others like to spend time late at night. Taking advantage of weekends and days off is also important. Throughout my personal journey and what I've seen from our members at Land Investing Online, its more about consistency than time. Moving the needle forward every day is better than random spurts of intense work. You will still need those random spurts, but most days will not be like that. Whether you put in twenty minutes one day and two hours the next day, it's about consistency. Once you get to the point where the business is up and running, you can quit your nine-to-five job and make this a full-time gig, or you can outsource and hire assistance to save you time and help you grow.

Markus Aurelius and the Stoic philosophers were big believers in taking consistent steps forward instead of the giant quantum leaps that society obsesses over. Take small wins every day and you'll look back in six months and see how far you come. One of my mentors said, "kill the rabbits, not the elephant," meaning you won't necessarily take down an elephant at once, but killing many rabbits will eventually be equivalent to the size of the elephant.

After staying consistent and putting in the work, you'll eventually notice a return on your investment. Like I mentioned in the previous section, putting these returns into the business is crucial. That's the way you'll see compounding growth and really start to take off.

When to Quit Your Nine-to-Five

Once you apply the principles this book covers, you will get to a point where you will likely be not only *able to* quit your job but will also *want to* . . . unless that job factors into your *why*. Let's say you make $100,000 from your job annually. After six months of land investing, let's say you're profiting $300,000 annually. In this case I would give yourself a reasonable salary, let's say $100,000. This still gives you $200,000 to reinvest into real estate deals, other investments, savings, etc. This is when I really see people take off. They are no longer worried about their marketing expenses or software subscriptions. Now that you have the mental freedom from worrying about your bills, you can aggressively, but smartly, reinvest your profits back into business.

Once you get to this point, you will need to make the decision to quit or not to quit your job(s). That comes down to a few things. First, is your job fulfilling, and does it fill your energy up instead of draining your energy? Second, are you able to get over the fear hump of quitting your stable job? I personally kept my job for much longer than I could have just for the safety aspect and the extra income. I did not have to pay myself a salary, get private insurance, or anything else that comes with being a full-time entrepreneur. But I will say, once I was able to put 100 percent of my focus into my entrepreneurship goals, my business quickly accelerated. When you finally make the leap, you'll see your passion and focus suddenly increase. Now for the first time ever, you are going to have to support yourself through your own business.

Let's look at James, who previously worked for a startup in California where he made great money but worked many hours and eventually burnt out. James came into the land investing space with the great mindset to continue to learn and dive deep into the industry. He was more conservative with his marketing, and it took him a little longer than average to get his feet under himself. But what James was great at doing was *learning*. He is one of the most knowledgeable land investors out there and that knowledge is a weapon that will help his career forever. James lived off of his savings and his wife's salary while he was diving into land space investing full time and was able to spend more time with his family and kids while doing so. After eight to twelve months James is making a great income and is a success at the land flipping game.

The difference is, James didn't have this as a side hustle at first—he dove right in and is now earning six-figures.

Now that you've heard about a few different journeys, it is important to realize that everyone's situation is unique. What works for one person might not be the right move for you. You have to analyze your situation and figure out what's best for you. These are real life examples of what entrepreneurship and real estate investing can do for you. Once your side hustle goes from a part-time income to enough to support yourself and your lifestyle, you'll know when to quit. There is no right or wrong answer on when to quit—it all is determined by the level of risk you're willing to take. Once you do quit your nine-to-five job, you'll experience the same freedom I saw, and you'll notice your focus and business start to takeoff. Don't worry, we go over, step by step, what you need to do later in this book to achieve these processes. I know you are not there yet, but you will be there very soon.

Invest, Invest, Invest

"The best investment you can make,
is an investment in yourself." —Warren Buffet.

Now that you're making loads of money and able to reinvest more into the process, continue to pour money into what's obviously working for you. You'll never get that good of a return off the stock market or conservative investments. Pour your resources into what is working now and watch it multiply, then when you still have extra capital, you can diversify your portfolio. Kevin O'Leary, the NBC's Shark Tank star and billionaire says, "You never put more than 20% in any one sector, and you never put more than 5% in any one stock."[3] By this he is saying he would never advise someone to put more than 20 percent of his net worth into real estate alone. But in my opinion, it is okay to grow a business by putting more than 20 percent in your pursuits. However, once you become wealthy, I agree with him that it is important to diversify your portfolio . . . at that point, invest in different stocks, real estate rental properties, crypto, commercial properties, bonds, funds, startups, and keep some cash on hand. Obviously as land investors we will be heavily skewed toward our land business but diversify that as much as possible. Diversification protects your wealth. If you need help, reach out to a financial advisor or mentor to guide you.

Wrap Up

This chapter hopefully has given you an idea of the path to financial freedom, finding your *why*, knowing when to quit your job, and achieving your dreams through consistent small steps. Being consistent is the number one way to make this work, and once you see the results it is important to reinvest more money into what is working. Remember, everyone's situation is different, and it is important to follow your specific journey.

---

3   Jayden Levitt, "Kevin O'Leary: If You Understand Modern Portfolio Theory, You'll Become Wealthy," March 29, 2023, https://jaydenlevitt. substack.com/p/kevin-oleary-if-you-understand-modern.

2
WHAT TO EXPECT

A few years ago, I remember making a call to my brother Ron to tell him about a great idea I had—land investing. I was so excited to tell him the idea and I remember I was driving from Cincinnati to a southeast Ohio cabin in a beautiful area called Hocking Hills. At this time I had already created and successfully operated seven-figure e-commerce stores and businesses so I knew the freedom entrepreneurship could bring. Ron, on the other hand, did not. He was working as a NCAA college basketball coach, working sixty to eighty hours per week, and constantly traveling. Although he seemed to love it, the money and freedom were not there. He knew he had to support his family and create a legacy for himself.

After our discussion Ron went home and researched the idea and concept. He immediately bought in and could envision what his future looked like. We got to work right away. Ron set a goal of making $50,000 his first year through land investing. Fast forward to two months later, together we'd made over ten times his goal.

Fast forward to two months later, and together, we'd made over ten times his goal. We had no idea how good this business would be to us. In just two months Ron had more freedom than ever and was now able to do the things he loved without worrying about a boss, location, or finances. Now Ron lives in Cincinnati, Ohio and loves spending time with his family, playing golf, watching sports, and more. He can enjoy himself and the money he is making by setting up his family for success. His wife even decided to quit her job so she could focus on raising their kids.

Understanding the Sacrifices

Before diving full force into the business, it is important to understand the sacrifices that come with it. Some people have greater sacrifices than others, depending on their unique situation. If you have a family, a job, and a lot of other commitments, some things will need to give. Time is limited, and you have to use your time wisely to make this work. Someone who has five kids, a nine-to-five job, and parents who need care will generally have less free time than a single twenty-two-year-old with very few commitments. In both scenarios, there will be sacrifices. For the single twenty-two-year-old, they may not be able to go out partying as often so they can save money and stay focused. For the person who has five kids, they may need to have a babysitter come three days a week so they can focus on the business while they're getting it up and running. Below are a few other examples of sacrifices one may face while starting a land flipping business.

- Less family time (temporarily).
- Less time with friends.

- Less eating out to save money.
- Less free time to do your hobbies.
- Less disposable income in order to reinvest in yourself.
- Increased workload—wake up earlier and stay up later.
- And much more.

Free Time

As I mentioned above, when Ron was a basketball coach, he had to use much of his free time for his new business. He knew this was temporary. You will still need personal free time and rest time, but if you're not consistently moving the needle forward, there will be little progress made. The key is to gain the momentum early and keep the momentum.

Hobbies

I am a big believer in hobbies. I do Brazilian jiu-jitsu, hangout with friends, hike, hunt, camp, and much more. I wouldn't be nearly as happy as I am today if it weren't for my hobbies. Keep your hobbies in your life but plan them out as much as possible to make sure you are balancing them with the necessary time to focus on investing. Make sure you are using *all* your time wisely. Once you're able to quit your nine-to-five and have extra time, things will get much easier. Plan ahead and use your calendar as much as you can for your hobbies and work.

Sleep Schedule

Now that you have a side hustle, you may need to adjust your sleep schedule. Rest and sleep are vital functions of health, and I focus on the quality and amount of sleep I get. When I was first starting my electric bike e-commerce store, I was waking up before my nine-to-five job to move the needle forward and get things done, some days by 5:00 a.m. and working from my bed to get things going. I was also working later than usual and taking full advantage of weekends. This is the only way to do it when you're first starting out. Anthony and Jeff, two members of Land Investing Online, have been meeting me every week for a call at 8:00 a.m. EST which is 5:00 a.m. PST! They are a part of every live call we hold and are extremely dedicated to the hustle. Like them, your sleep schedule may need to adjust a bit in order to get your work done, but remember, these are temporary adjustments you're making for the future of your life. It's worth it. I promise.

Friends

John C. Maxwell said, "The better you are at surrounding yourself with people of high potential, the greater your chance for success." This quote has meant so much to me, and I have seen this personally affect my life in profound ways. As a committed entrepreneur, you have an obligation to keep refining your peer group so they add value to your goals, values, and outcomes. This can work both ways. If you are surrounded by negative people who don't believe in you, it weighs on you and affects you in a negative way. Take a deep look at your closest friends to see who has a positive or a negative effect on you. Though difficult, this can be a very eye-opening experience.

In Ed Mylett's book *The Power of One More*, he talks about your relationship's bullseye. Think of your relationships as a series of concentric circles like a bullseye. Each circular space represents different intimacy levels of the people you encounter. The closer you get to the center, the closer you get to the people who connect with you on a deeper level. Mylett states that the outer ring is for the strangers you meet, perhaps people sitting next to you in the bar or people you pass on a daily basis. It could even be the cold-caller calling you about that extended car warranty! In general, the impact the outer ring and these strangers make on you is minimal. The next ring would be acquaintances or people you see from time to time—like your kids' teachers, the butcher at your local deli, or random interactions with people at the gym. These are closer to your bullseye and have some impact on you, but not a tremendous amount. The innermost circle is small and consists of just a few people who impact you daily, like your spouse, parents, children, and friends, etc. Your inner circle could have a mentor, business partner, or just a friend you click with. You are at the center of all these circles. You are the bullseye. The nature of life is that people enter your circle and move closer or further away from that bulls-eye over time, all a natural part of life.

Regularly take a closer look at your inner circle of friends. Think about all the small groups of friends you're closest to in your life. Who are the few people you spend the most time with outside of your family? Do these people have a few things in their life such as traits, emotions, fitness levels, success, spirituality that you want in your life? Are these people pushing you closer to your dreams or steering you away from them? Do you talk to them and feel energized? If these people don't have anything in their life that you want, you may need to search for some new friends. When analyzing your friends, remind yourself it is always *quality over quantity*. A small amount of time spent with the right people can make a big difference. You learn from one another and fuel each other's mental battery.

Like I mentioned above, everyone will have different sacrifices they need to make in order to stay focused, save money, and pour their resources into their business. For me personally, I had to wake up early to get work done. I also had to answer phone calls throughout the day. My workload increased exponentially while I was trying to learn and execute the business. My evenings were spent learning as much as possible. Since I was an outside salesman, I was listening to YouTube and podcasts all day long trying to absorb all the information I could. I became obsessed with the business and was willing to do anything to make it work, which is the mindset you should have. It will be temporary, and once you get your business off the ground and running, you can ease up. Just remember, the first six months are the hardest.

Investing in Yourself

As we briefly touched on previously, investing in yourself is crucial to your overall entrepreneurial success. Investing in yourself now will continue to multiply as time goes on, and the combination of time and money will work in your favor. As you start to see more and more success, look to make your business more efficient by hiring employees, implementing new software, etc. We will discuss hiring and outsourcing more later on in the book, but this is a great place to start when you have extra funds so you can delegate tasks to an employee while you focus on moving the business forward.

Invest in your business financially and invest in yourself personally. Your personal and professional life correlate intimately. The more you are fulfilled and happy in life the more your business will feed off that. Knowing that, make sure to invest time in the gym, on your hobbies, health, diet, etc. As you go down the rabbit hole of entrepreneurship, it is important to keep up your health and mental happiness. It is easy to lose sight of that, but I can't express how important it is. I've personally been in very dark places throughout my entrepreneurship journey, and I can tell you right now that my businesses suffered during those tough times. Looking back, my businesses have always flourished and prospered when I was feeling and acting my best.

Invest time and energy into yourself.

Overcoming Fear

Fear is without a doubt the number one reason people fail in entrepreneurship and business. Most people who fail never really gave it consistent time and energy. A common way I see people "fail" in land investing is by doing it for fifteen to twenty days and then stopping to see if they get results. Anytime you stop, you raise the chances of failure. The people who succeed are the ones who are relentless with consistency. It is scary investing in yourself and spending all this money on something you don't know is going to work, but as I stated earlier, land flipping is a proven business model. It does work. It comes down to execution. The truth is that people who fail tend to stop after day fifteen because they are scared to continue, scared of the unknown, and scared to put money into investing in their future.

Franklin D. Roosevelt said, "The only thing we have to fear is fear itself." Fear can be an extreme paralyzer, causing inaction and a lack of growth. People who push through fear and the uncomfortable times are the happiest and most successful. Constantly overcoming fear is a great way to find fulfillment and success. If you do this consistently, something you fear today will no longer be a fear in six months. An example of this is public speaking, one of the world's most common fears. Say you had to go around to one hundred different universities to give speeches to large audiences. Do you think you will be as scared on the hundredth presentation as you were on the first? Absolutely not. That is because you overcame the fear by taking action and getting comfortable with uncomfortable situations. Take this ideology and apply it to every aspect of life. Overcoming fear and doing hard things actually makes you happy because it builds confidence and because it is about the journey not the destination. Once you do something extremely hard and beat it, you will feel fulfilled beyond belief. Sitting around all day not pushing yourself causes lack of fulfilment and depression. The key to happiness is in the journey.

Focus

Cutting out the noise and staying focused is crucial for success. Some of your friends, family, and other acquaintances will doubt you and tell you what you're doing won't work. All that doubt and negativity needs to be cut out. It's nothing more than a distraction. Yes, your parents usually want the best for you, but they are not always right. You must find a way to distance these people if they are causing you to lose focus and doubt the process. Your brain and energy need to be wrapped around the process and force that negativity into motivation.

Let me tell you my story about this phenomenon. I had a horrible GPA in high school and didn't get admitted to any colleges at first. My high school teachers and administrators doubted that I would ever do anything with my life. I could feel and sense this doubt. But I was able to turn that doubt into motivation. I was determined to prove them wrong. So what if I didn't excel in school; a report card is only one measure of talent and success. I was confident I could do so much more. I cut out their negativity from my life so I could focus on what I wanted, but I used that memory to motivate me. To this day, their doubts provide me with the motivation to succeed and prove the world wrong. Although this is not my primary motivation, it still helps me. But by eliminating negative distractions, cutting out doubt and noise, and staying laser-focused I was able to succeed in business. And not just one . . . all of them.

When starting your entrepreneurial journey, you have to be 100 percent dedicated to the process. *Cut through all the noise.*

Phases of Business

Early on in one of my early businesses, Urban Bikes Direct, I ran into a *major* roadblock. To simplify a long story, banks and credit card processing companies classified the business as high risk and wouldn't accept me. But before telling me that, they automatically opened up my account to accept payments from customers while my account was under review. So like any normal business, I could accept credit cards. The problem was that after my business was reviewed, they shut me down and would no longer accept any orders. But I had already accepted tens of thousands of dollars of orders and shipped them out, therefore paying for the inventory. The processing companies told me I wouldn't receive my funds for six months. This put major financial stress on me that I had never experienced, before or since. I did not know how I would stay afloat.

When I got that call from the processing company saying they could not release my money, my heart dropped. I didn't quite understand it and I thought there would be a way to get my money out. PayPal did the same exact thing to me. All in all, I had tens of thousands of dollars locked. I eventually found a processing company that would work with me. I had $30,000 in credit card debt and tens of thousands of dollars locked up with the processors. I didn't know how long the business would survive. This is what I eventually would call my breaking point. Every business will face this to some degree at some point. Whether it be shutting down due to a pandemic, having to fire employees, being scared to take that next step, or something else, business in general is always a series of ups and downs.

As you see in the graph below from *Business Insider*, business growth fluctuates. One key point to notice is your last bottom is higher than the next bottom and your next peak is higher than the previous peak. To put this into simpler terms, progress isn't a straight line. It's a series of ups and downs and over time it is up. It is important to know this while you're going through a breaking point. It is easy to be happy and fulfilled when everything is going well, but how will you react when you're at a breaking point?

The phases of a business cycle
follow a wave-like pattern over time

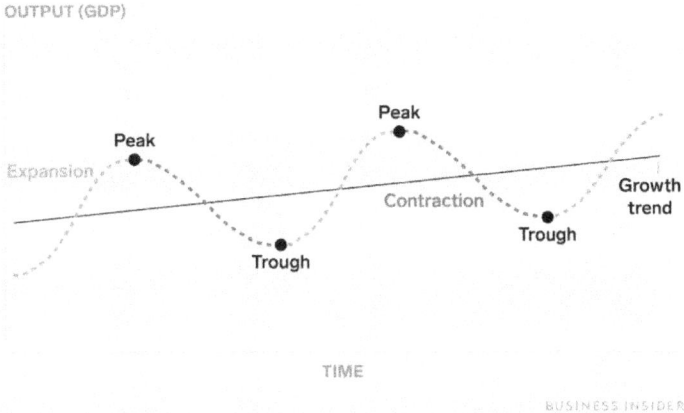

OUTPUT (GDP)

Peak

Peak

Expansion

Contraction

Growth
trend

Trough

Trough

TIME

BUSINESS INSIDER

4

When you're in a breaking point, you must analyze the situation from a non-emotional state. Some breaking points are much worse than others. One of our members went into $12,000 of credit card debt with no plans to pay it off if it failed. He also had a family to support. His lows were going to be much lower than someone who was making $150,000 at their job and could afford to lose money. As I described earlier in the book, Mike was a great example. I remember when he called me to quit. He said things weren't working and he was going to apply for other nine-to-five jobs to make more money. It was only three weeks later that

4   Ali Hussain, "Business Cycles Chart the Ups and Downs of an Economy, and Understanding Them Can Lead to Better Financial Decisions," Business Insider, August 27, 2020, https://www. businessinsider.in/finance/news/business-cycles-chart-the-ups-and-downs-of-an-economy-and-understanding-them-can-lead-to-better-financial-decisions/articleshow/77793878.cms.

he called me excited to tell me about all the momentum he was now getting. A few months later, Mike had six properties under contract that will net him more money than that other job would have. Fast forward to today: Mike has over $1 million in properties listed for sale, making him hundreds of thousands of dollars.

Some breaking points may last a few days, others a few weeks, and some will take months or years. It all comes down to your goals, vision, and mission—that is ultimately what gets you through those times. For me, I think about how I want to be remembered and the lives I can positively affect. For Mike, he thinks about quitting his nine-to-five job and having money to go on vacations with his family, buy a nice house with a big yard, and go to all the sporting events he wants to. Breaking points and obstacles are inevitable. The best thing I can offer you is to be prepared for them and know you're not alone. Moving through them with awareness of them is the best thing to do.

One of my mentors, Joe Sheehey, founder of *Cured Nutrition*, has talked a lot about his business in 2019, which was on the verge of collapsing, and how he had to completely create new systems, processes, and core values to get through the tough times. It got to the point where he wasn't sleeping at night and was scared his business would go under. Little did he know, just one year later his business would be valued over $10 million. There's not one successful entrepreneur out there that hasn't moved through a breaking point.

Developing the Right Attributes

"I deconstructed grit into four component attributes: courage, perseverance, adaptability and resilience."
—Rich Diviney, *The Attributes*

In the book *The Attributes,* Rich Diviney developed the idea of attributes as a means of better selecting candidates for intensive Navy SEAL training after realizing that assessing for skills was not useful. Rich quickly realized skills like shooting, driving, languages, and others, could be taught. The SEALs were actually selecting for attributes which are more innate and would determine how a person will react to uncertainty, challenges, and stress. These same laws apply to business. Skills like accounting, updating spreadsheets, sales calls, customer service and other daily tasks can be taught. Rich argues that skills are what it takes to make a business successful, but things like grit—broken down into four attributes labeled courage, perseverance, adaptability, and resilience—is what keeps entrepreneurs moving forward during tough times. As I mentioned earlier in this book, it wasn't my high school or college degree that got me to where I am today. It was more about me pushing through my fear by using my personal traits of resilience. Let's look at the four attributes related to grit below.

- **Courage**: The ability to manage fear in order to confront danger, difficulty, or pain.
- **Perseverance**: Constancy doing something despite difficulty or delay in achieving success.

- **Adaptability**: The ability to quickly and calmy adjust to changing circumstances and situations.
- **Resilience**: The ability to rapidly return to one's baseline emotional and mental state after a stressful, traumatic, or even triumphant event.

Now read over those definitions again while thinking of how they can relate to entrepreneurship. If someone has courage, they are going to be able to take the leaps when needed. Fear is not holding them back; they trust the process and their instinct. If someone has perseverance, they'll be able to get through the hard work and continue to push forward even though results are delayed, which they almost always are in business. Someone who can adapt will be better equipped for the external changes that happen. In the most recent scenario, think of COVID-19 and how businesses had to adapt. That is an extreme example that virtually happened over night, but things like changes in technology and consumer behavior change slower over time. If one is resilient, they can get through the extremely tough times in life and in business and can quickly bounce back while continuing to move the business forward.

Grit is not the only attribute that matters in business, but someone who has these traits will succeed much more often than not. From my coaching experience, the ones who succeed are the ones who continue to move forward despite hard times, the ones who push through fear and the ones who are okay with having delayed gratification. Success does not happen overnight; it takes a long time of consistency before you reach the freedom you're looking for.

Identifying Purpose and Goals

Identifying your specific purpose and goals is critical to success. It is easy to have the motivation and drive when things are great. It's easy when it's a beautiful 75 degree day with no clouds in the sky. But what happens when things get difficult? How do you mentally overcome the difficult circumstances that will arise? When times get tough it is important to imagine you quitting your job and remind yourself of why you are doing this in the first place. What does that freedom look and feel like?

Wrap Up

It is true there are sacrifices associated with entrepreneurship and land investing. It is also important to understand the rewards that come from those sacrifices. You may need to temporarily change some of your habits—your sleep schedule, hobbies, friends, and more. You have to find the time to do the work, and you'll have to surround yourself with the right people while doing so. But once you have steady income and are financially free, things will get easier.

3

UNLOCKING YOUR FREEDOM WITH LAND INVESTING

Land investing has provided me more freedom than any of the other ten-plus business models I have been a part of. That is simply because of the profit potential of the business and the long term sustainability of the business. I recently recorded a podcast episode called "Will Land Investing be Here in 50 Years?" The answer to this question is *yes*. The way we may do business will of course change, but the bare bones of buying property at under-market value and reselling it will stay the same. How we buy properties, the techniques and other aspects I can't even yet image, will change, as any business does over time, but for me personally, that is a huge part of the freedom. Knowing that I can do this forever and not worry about how I am going to make a living in a few years is incredibly freeing.

Land investing is the process of buying vacant lots for under market value and reselling them for market value. As of now, we acquire these properties through direct mail with offer letters included without ever having seen the property in person—a process known as a blind offer. We also have acquired properties through texting and cold calling, which we will dive into later in the book. Blind offers have been the most efficient way we've found to acquire under-market-value land, which is why we will spend a lot of time on that subject. It is the combination of both blind offers and texting or cold calling that works best.

Let's look at an example:

- We select to send mail to Hamilton County, Ohio based on our research.
- Our data shows we need to target properties from five to twenty acres.

Based on the information above, we will send an offer letter to anyone in Hamilton County, Ohio who owns vacant land from five to twenty acres. It might say, "Hi James, we are interested in purchasing your five-acre parcel in Hamilton County, Ohio for $50,000. If you are interested in this offer, the second page of this agreement has a legal offer letter on it to sign and get the process started." Obviously, there is much more detail than that, but that covers the basics of how we buy the land. We typically offer between 35 – 50 percent of market value. It's a numbers game, and it only takes one person to say yes to make this work.

You may be asking, why would anyone want to sell for 35 – 50 percent of market value? The answer is simple. Quick cash is king. If someone needs a quick way out of their land for whatever reason, we are the solution. Medical bills, layoffs, recessions, or just being tired of paying taxes are all reasons why people choose to sell to us. We operate based on the idea of convenience—a quick way to solve financial issues with a closing within two weeks.

Why wouldn't the buyer just list with a Realtor? There are multiple reasons, but typically it takes a long time, and you still don't know what the property is going to sell for. The Realtor then takes a commission, and the seller has to account for the six months it took to sell. If someone wants and needs money *now*, we have a great solution and an easy way out.

We have a way to assess a price based on what we think the properties in that acreage range will sell for on the market. We then take the retail value and come up with a price we want to offer. We will talk more about this in the next chapter. Once we buy the land, we market it and resell it for close to market value. For us, our average time on the market is around three weeks. We put it on the local Multiple Listing Service (MLS), so it is on Zillow, Redfin, Realtor.com and all the other sites associated with the MLS. We also list it on Facebook Marketplace, Craigslist, Land.com and other sources. We make sure to do a very good job with pictures and descriptions in order for it to sell quickly. If priced appropriately and marketed in the correct areas, the property will sell quickly.

In the following chapters we will go over how we do each step of the process and share how many of our first-year members earn over $250,000. This income level is not easy to reach, but it is absolutely possible. For now, let's briefly look into the various methods of real estate investing and how they compare to land investing. Below we will compare some of the largest real estate niches, such as rental properties, house flipping, and wholesaling.

Real Estate Investing Methodologies

As a rental real estate investor myself, commonly known as buy-and-hold real estate investing, this one really hits the spot. When we are talking about traditional real estate investing, much of what we do revolves around structures like houses, commercial properties, multi-family, and more. With structures come problems—difficult tenants, renovations, upkeep, and repairs, etc., etc. I've had to evict tenants and deal with all the headaches traditional real estate can cause. I personally love my rental properties, but it is not by any means simple or easy. My goal is not to talk you out of rental investments. I still actively seek and buy them myself—but it is not my full-time income, and I do it for long-term wealth, diversification, and the tax benefits. But they can be timely and costly.

In land investing, we like to use the "Ts" to describe the simplicity: no Tenants, no Termites, and no Toilets! When buying and selling land you do not need to deal with any county permits. There are no building code regulations to consider. Let's face it, no one wants to deal with the county and city regulations. We are selling dirt. Dirt is simple, and simple means fewer headaches. With the land investing strategy we discuss in this book, we are seeking less hassle and more simplicity.

Rental Properties Versus Land Investing

When I graduated from college, I knew I wanted to get into real estate. I thought the right path was through rentals, but I quickly learned that was not the ideal path for my situation. I feel, as many others do, that rental properties are a path to quitting your nine-to-five job, but I think only for a certain group of people. In this section I will discuss the pros and cons of rentals versus land flipping, along with who the ideal person is for the niche.

Rental Investing Pros and Cons

Pros:

- Great long term investment.
- Stable and safe – this method has been around for a long time and is very safe relative to a lot of other businesses.
- Equity – Rentals appreciate in value and, over the course of five to ten years, your property value could double if you buy in the right areas.
- Tax benefits – the government gives benefits, such as depreciation, for rental properties.
- Low risk.

Cons

- Low cash flow – Due to its safety, the cash flow returns are less than many other models of real estate investing. Much of the earning potential is in the equity in the property. Each property is different, but don't expect to make thousands each month from your rental property. It takes a lot of units for it to add up.
- Income delay – It takes a long time to see the benefits from the rental property. By the time you buy the property, rehab it, get tenants placed, and see returns, it can take up to a year. Even after that, the cash flow is still low, so much of your income potential is through the property's equity, which takes time to grow.

- Upfront capital needed – It typically costs a fair chunk of change to buy a property if you have a down payment of 20 – 30 percent.
- Loans – Dealing with rental properties, you typically need to leverage debt. Debt can bring you up or pull you down, and it also comes with a tremendous amount of risk. In land investing, you won't need to leverage debt like this. We have a process where you can get financing for your loans without a credit score or being underwritten.

Overall, I love rental properties but if you are looking for a way out of your nine-to-five this is not the best move for you. I personally like to take my extra income from land investing and diversify by putting it into rental properties for the benefits above. When you're talking ten- to thirty-year investments, it does not get much better than good rental properties. But the biggest thing you have to know here is that the income will not come quickly.

House Flipping Versus Land Investing

House flipping has taken off in the last several years due to HGTV and the fancy flipping shows that get everyone excited. I have nothing against the shows and many of them are quite entertaining, but it has created a huge demand for people looking to flip properties.

House Flipping Pros and Cons
Pros:
- Immediate income opportunity.
- Sustainable and will not go anywhere.

Cons:
- Highly competitive.
- Generally tight margins.
- Requires county and city permits.
- Requires heavy management with contractors.
- Upfront capital and loans.
- High risk.

Personally, in the state of today's market, I am not a huge fan of house flipping. I think it would make much more sense to buy a property under market value that needs a lot of work, fix it up, and then rent it. You can then refinance it and get your money out while still retaining the asset you worked so hard for. It is such a competitive industry and dealing with contractors, permits, and all the other hassles can be exhausting. One of the main reasons why I love land investing is because you're not working with any contractors, and you don't need any permits or government permission. There is definitely money to be made in flipping houses, but with the high level of competition, it makes fix-and-flip properties extremely hard to come across. Once you find one, you then have the hassle of working with a local hard money lender to come up with a loan that fits your needs. So if you're looking for fewer headaches, house flipping is not the way to go.

Wholesaling Versus Land Investing

Traditional real estate wholesaling is where you find a property that the owner wants to sell, and then find a buyer for that property. For example, say I found that Bill wants to sell his house at 123 Curby Lane for $100,000. I then go to a group of investors I know and send them the information on the property and see who wants to buy it for $120,000. I then pocket the $20,000 as my commission for finding and brokering the deal. That's how wholesalers make money. My selling point to investors is the house may be worth $160,000, so ideally both sides get what they want. The buyer gets to sell quickly, the wholesaler makes $20,000, and the investors have the potential to either hold the property or make $40,000+ selling it later. Generally these properties need extensive work and improvements due to the condition they are in.

Wholesaling Pros and Cons

Pros:

- Low Risk – not much capital needed.
- Immediate income potential – it should not take too long for you to make income using this method.

Cons

- Very competitive industry.
- Can be difficult to find sellers.
- Heavily dependent on a buyer's list of investors.
- Restrictions on listing the property to the public.
- Less value to sellers.
- Can get shady if you're not transparent.

Wholesaling can be a good place to start because it can get you out of your nine-to-five job fairly quickly without too much upfront capital. The problem, however, is that it is highly competitive. It can be very hard to find good deals, especially when you are not buying the property yourself. You must go to your group of investors and find a buyer for the property, which can scare a lot of people off from selling their property. Also, since you do not own the property, you cannot list it publicly and sell it on the MLS (Zillow, Redfin, Realtor.com). That is why having a solid list of investors who will buy the properties is so crucial to this business.

Meanwhile, in land investing, we own the property so we can list it on all the sites and can sell them quickly and for around full value. Wholesalers have to sell well below market value because they need to be able to get an investor to buy it, who then also needs a way to make money. In my experience, land investing has been much more profitable and sustainable due to the fact we are able to sell the property to the public, not to investors, but there are wholesalers in land who do fairly well. In fact, later in this book we will talk about a strategy known as double closing, which is very similar to wholesaling. The margins are tighter when you do this, but there are occasions when it is worth trying.

Wrap Up

While considering different methods of real estate, it is important to understand the pros and cons of each method and how they fit into your financial goals and your *why*. For me personally, my goal was to get out of my nine-to-five job through a lucrative and cash-flow-heavy business model. Land investing was perfect for that. Now I take my profit and invest in long-term rentals for steady appreciation, tax incentives, and a little cash flow. Land investing as a business provides incredible opportunity for those looking for a way to get your freedom, quit your job, and experience a meaningful and fulfilling life.

4

LAND INVESTING OVERVIEW

Why Land Investing?

One of the most common questions I am asked is, "How much money can I make from land investing?" There is no simple answer to that. Land investing is an extremely attractive business because of the low upfront costs, its sustainability, and its profitability. Land investing can also be done well in any market: when it's a slower market, then we buy cheaper, and if it's a hot market, then we buy higher. Just in the last few years, we went from a historic hot market, post-COVID, to one that is starting to cool off. I have had to adapt this business model to be just as profitable in both hot and cold markets. In this chapter, we will discuss the variables at play as well as the upfront costs associated with the business model.

Sustainability

Sustainability is a topic that is so easily overlooked. When analyzing different businesses, you should first start to look at the business from a long-term perspective. Think in terms of twenty to thirty years instead of three years. Yes, selling fidget spinners may have been a great idea in 2013, but the businesses that focused solely on that one product were out of business by 2015. It's not only about what makes you money *now*, but also what makes you money *ten years from now*. When you build a well-planned, sustainable business you're building a long-term asset that you can eventually sell. Land investing is no different.

The first thing to do is create a plan. Do the work to figure out what you're going to do today, a month from now, a year from now, and five years from now. This isn't just about goals, it's more about creating some sort of a business plan. And then determine your strategy for meeting those goals in the specific market you identified for your business plan. Finally, you can get into the nitty-gritty of determining your offer structure.

So how do we come up with our offers? We typically offer a percentage of what we anticipate the market value to be. For example, take a five-acre plot in Douglas County, WA. Our data may show us it is valued at $50,000. We will send letters with an offer for that property to landowners in that county for somewhere between $18,000 – $25,000. Determining that number is what we will dive into in more detail throughout this chapter. Many people, when they first hear about this approach, will ask why anyone would ever sell property for less than half of what it's worth. Here are the main reasons:

1. **Raw land is difficult to price.** With very few comps in rural America, there is less data available to support a specific price. It is not like residential real estate where you know a three-bedroom, 1500-square-foot house will sell for $250,000 in a specific neighborhood because there are twenty comps within a mile supporting that. With land investing, you may not have a good comp for twenty miles or more. This makes the data analytics side extremely difficult and especially crucial to the process. Many landowners don't know the value of their own land.

   The hardest thing to do in this business is evaluate land, so we have to become experts in it. I cannot tell you how many times I've asked a Realtor's opinion on what a piece of land is worth, and they were 50 – 80 percent off my own assessment. This shows how difficult it can be. This is also where the risk in this business comes in. There are market fluctuations and numerous unknowns. So even when I assess a property at a number, I know I could be 20 percent off myself. This is a business, and I have to offer a price that accounts for those fluctuations and still be able to make a profit. Landowners often know that and understand the difficulties. They avoid the pain of that uncertainty that I assume, but the cost of that is making less than they could have if they sold their properties themselves.

2. **Land is hard to sell.** Through years of experience, we have learned how to properly sell land on the market. Our formula (that we will get to later) will show you how to market and sell your property fast! It boils down to this: we list land at the appropriate price and in the appropriate places. About 70 – 80 percent of land listings online are overpriced and won't sell. Putting your property for sale at the right price is the first and most critical step. Because landowners don't know the value of their land, and often don't want to learn how to do it, they are willing to sacrifice some profit to avoid it. On top of that, we get them money in just a couple weeks without the risk of the property sitting on the market for months and months until they get paid.

3. **Many Realtors don't know land and don't want to list land.** There are few Realtors in rural America, so when they get a call to list a $40,000 property that is two hours away from them, they have to ask themselves if it is worth the money. It's often not. Realtors are paid on commission and prefer high-end houses that will make them more money. Since there's not as much money in land as there is in properties with structures, there are fewer Realtors who actually know what they are talking about when it comes to land. And as we've already mentioned, there are very few comps for Realtors to analyze. Without qualified Realtors, landowners are often left with few choices other than selling to investors or learning how to manage the process themselves.

4. **Many landowners have never been to their land or never used it.** About 50 percent of the land my firm buys is from people who have never even been to the land they own. Often, they have inherited it and live out of the area. Easy and fast is often more important to them than getting full value. So we make it very easy on the sellers and provide the contract for them to sign and send right back to us via text, email, or fax. If they are in a precarious financial situation and need $50,000 to pay off debts—cars, mortgage, tuition or whatever it may be—you're in the right place at the right time.

5. **Cash offers and quick closes.** We typically close our purchases within two weeks of getting the property under contract. In some areas we do it in three days! We are buying this in our own names and not wholesaling or assigning the contract to anyone else. That is why our offers work so well. When a landowner gets a contract in the mail for $50,000 and they can have their money in ten days, it gets their attention if they need or want the money at that time. We provide an enormous amount of value to sellers who want the sale done quickly for any number of reasons. If a landowner wanted to sell their property on the market, they would take on the risk of it not selling, as well as the risk that it will take months or years to sell and finally provide their profit.

It's a mutually beneficial arrangement, and hearing some of the stories from sellers about how we helped them is extremely gratifying.

Upfront Costs

Earlier, I said that one of the reasons land investing is lucrative is due to the low upfront costs to close your first deal. That does not mean there aren't some costs. When I got started, I didn't have tens of thousands of dollars to invest in a service business. I had to find something economical. Let's be real, businesses traditionally need very hefty upfront investments to get started. How is someone without that capital supposed to get started?

That's why I originally got started in online business and entrepreneurship, and then moved on to land investing. The upfront capital needed to get started is very minimal compared to traditional business models. When I got started in land investing, we did not put much of our upfront capital in the business. We utilized our money for marketing and mail. We utilized other people's money for actually purchasing the land, a.k.a. deal funding. Yes, that meant we lost some profit, but we were able to leverage other money to spend on getting more deals.

The biggest expense in this business model is mail. Mail, at the current time of writing this book, is seventy cents or more for each letter, envelope, and stamp. We typically recommend investors start by having $3,000 to $5,000 for mailing, which is much less than many traditional business and other real estate models. Once you start making returns and seeing the business model actually work, you will start investing more and more into mail and marketing.

When you get your first property under contract, you can partner up with another land investor to fund the deal and you split the profit. In traditional real estate, this is known as a joint venture (JV). In this case, you brought value from finding the deal, and the funder brought value from providing the money. In the end, you work out a profit split that we will go into later in this book.

If you are starting with $5,000, that should give you the ability to send roughly seven thousand units of mail. That should yield you multiple deals if you do it right. There are a few other upfront costs as well, like data. You will need to purchase the records from a data service site. These data services will spit out records based on the criteria you select. We use one called The Land Portal. My brother Ron and I developed The Land Portal because the industry was missing a great data solution for land investors. However, there other data services out there that you can use.

Other than mail and data, all other costs are very minimal. While we recommend people have between $3,000 to $5,000 to begin, you can have more or less than that to start. So don't get stressed out! It is only a recommendation, and you should go with your own comfort level regarding your starting investment.

It's also important to note that there are some alternative marketing methods you can use that can be less expensive than mail. But they can also be less effective. We will discuss those later in this book. If you are using these other methods, you will not need the original $3,000 – $5,000 to get started; that price is based on the mail marketing method that my company teaches, which is what we have found to be by far the most efficient and effective way to acquire land.

How to Pay For Deals

People think that since we are buying land, we need to have enough money to pay for our mail *and* our deals. Our average land purchase is around $20,000 and we don't expect the average person to be able to purchase this themselves. There are alternative methods to paying for your deals yourself. As previously mentioned, the most commonly used method is called "deal-funding", or finding a partner to put up the money for the purchase. In the end, you decide on the profit split. Once you start networking in the land community you will notice how easy it is to get your deals funded. There are a lot of deal funders because of the cycle of a land investor. Once you send mail consistently and are buying and selling properties, you will have excess cash. Once you have excess capital, you will want to place that capital somewhere where it can work for you. You only have so many deals you can purchase yourself, and you now have the ability to pay for your own deals and pay for other people's deals. Paying for other people's deals is extremely attractive because you take a good profit split without doing any of the work. You don't need to find the deal and manage the deal through the whole buying and selling process.

If you do fund your initial deals yourself, you'll likely still need to deal fund eventually. You might currently have $50,000 and think you can fund all of your deals yourself. But what happens when you get one deal that costs $48,000, then you get another that costs $25,000 that same week? You will always run out of funds if you're growing. Funding deals yourself is a great way to maximize profit without giving away a big piece of the pie, but you will need to leverage other money at some point.

Profitability

Everyone wants to know how much money you can make in land investing, and to be honest, that was one of the most attractive parts of land investing for me when I first got started. While you can research the average income for an investor all you want, at the end of the day the possibilities are endless. This is a business model that can scale. If you want to keep it a one man show, that is completely fine. If you want to hire employees and scale up your business, that is great. Everyone has different aspirations. For me, I wanted to outsource and build a sustainable business that did not need me to operate. In order to do that I had to devote a lot of my time to management and growth rather than just land investing. It's quite a big mindset shift when going from a one man show to hiring and outsourcing. But if you want to make a great income without hiring, this is a great business model, too. You can get a virtual assistant to help take care of your backend work to help free some of your time. And you'll make a great profit there too, just at a different rate than if you'd outsourced.

That's why when someone asks the question, "How much money can you make land investing?" there is no correct answer. I've seen people make millions of dollars with very few to no employees. I also know some people who do it at a much smaller scale and do a deal or two on the side every few months. There is no limit to the income you can make in this business model. This book will teach you the fundamentals and strategies behind it. What you do after it is up to you.

Average Profit Per Deal

When starting my land investing career, the majority of my deals were on the smaller side. The first property I ever bought was for $6,000 and I sold it the same week for $15,000. Although I still love getting those deals, we do many bigger ones. I recently listed a property I bought for $200,000 for $480,000. That is on the larger end for my business. When it comes to our average, we usually buy for around $20,000 to $30,000 and sell between $40,000 to $65,000. Our average profit per deal is around $23,000 in 2022. We see that number trending up with some of the bigger deals we are doing now, but we still love the simplicity and consistency of the smaller deals. The smaller deals keep the pipeline full and then we sprinkle in bigger deals naturally over time.

There really are *no limits*.

Profit Per Mail Campaign

Based on our data, we currently acquire one property per every two thousand pieces of mail we send out. That puts our cost per acquisition at about $1,300 on average and our average profit is about $24,000. So for every two thousand mailers we send out, we know we will get $23,000 back. Keep in mind, this is profit without any deal financing or interest. If you use a partner to fund the deal, you'll have to give them a piece of the pie.

It's also important to note that these results are based on an analysis of the hundreds of thousands of mailers we've sent out. Our sample size is very large and yours will not be, at least not at first. I see many people come to us trying to analyze their results after only sending four thousand pieces of mail. Yes, if you're doing it right, four thousand mailers *should* yield a deal. But it does not always play out that cleanly. Sometimes four thousand mailers will get you nothing and the next four thousand will get you five deals. We once sent 1,200 pieces of mail to an area and got over ten deals back, thus netting over $500,000 in profit in just a couple months! On the flip side, we have sent five thousand mailers with zero results. It's a numbers game and the most important part is staying consistent with your mail and not over-analyzing. Keeping the marketing and mail flowing consistently will yield the best results.

Now that you know a little bit about the price per deal, let's talk about annual income to expect. The amount of income you make is a result of the amount of mail you send. It sounds simple, right? Mail is expensive and the only thing holding people back is themselves and the fear of spending more money on mail. If we use the equation above, expecting to acquire one deal for every two thousand pieces of mail, we can work backward from there. Say we send five thousand pieces of mail per month for twelve months. From that equation, we know we will yield about thirty deals on average. Thirty deals multiplied by our current average profit per deal is $660,000. Subtract your marketing expenses, deal financings, and deal funding expenses and you will be well into the six figures!

This seems simple, but that does not mean it's *easy*. Staying consistent with five thousand mailers per month requires a lot of dedication and hard work. Let's dive into this example further.

$$5,000 \text{ (Units of Mail)}$$
$$\times 12 \text{ (Months)}$$

$$60,000 \text{ (Units of Mail)}$$
$$\div 2,000 \text{ (Average Mail to Acquire One Property)}$$

$$30 \text{ (Deals)}$$
$$\times \$22,000 \text{ (Average Profit)}$$

$$\$660,000$$
$$- \$42,000 \text{ (Mail and Marketing Expenses)}$$
$$- \$264,000 \text{ (Funding Profit Split)}$$

$$\$354,000 \text{ (Profit)}$$

In the situation above, I used a funding profit split of 40 percent of your net profit. That only applies if you are using a funding partner for every single deal. I encourage you to purchase as many of these yourself as you build up your cash situation to help drive down your costs per deal.

Niches

Finding a niche can be crucial for long-term success and sustainability in land investing. You might be thinking that land itself *is* a niche. Although that is correct, there is much more to it. Within land purchases, there are specific niches you can become involved in. Here are some that I've seen people focus on:

- Tax sale properties.
- Landlocked properties (land without access).
- Probate properties (needing to go to probate court).
- Commercial lots.
- Mobile home lots.
- Infill lots (empty plots in an urban or developed area).
- Mastering one specific geographic market.
- Recreational land and hunting properties.

I don't expect you to know what all the niches above mean, but you will get to know them with more time in real estate and land investing. Each of these niches has its own challenges, and with those challenges comes varying degrees of profit and sustainability. The harder something is to master, the harder it is for competition to come in. Once you develop a niche, you will become an expert in it, and this experience and local knowledge are valuable; they give you leverage to close deals ahead of your competition. But niches are nothing to force. They typically come naturally with time. I do not recommend exploring a niche early on, but after you get your feet wet, it is something to keep in mind as you progress in this industry.

Deal Flow

Deal flow is another very important part of this business. Think of what your pipeline will look like. You send the mail out, get the property under contract, send the property to escrow, buy the property, list it for sale, sell it, and repeat. You need deals in each of these stages at all times to make consistent money. You don't want all of your deals in escrow at once and none for sale or none that you are buying. That means you will have a massive pause in your income. You make money when you sell the property, so you want to constantly be selling. In order to sell, you have to go through all of the other steps. Below is what a healthy deal flow pipeline looks like:

Pipeline Stage	# of Properties
Negotiation	6
Due Diligence	4
Purchasing/Escrow	5
For Sale	6
Sell-side Escrow	4

Did you notice how all of those phases of the process are fairly even? That is a very healthy deal flow. The properties move through each phase, and it is important to never have any of the phases completely dry. At first, it is not as important, but over time you really want to focus on deal flow if you are doing this for a full time living. Below is what your deal flow will look like early on, which is fine at the beginning, but it becomes unhealthy as time goes on.

Pipeline Stage	# of Properties
Negotiation	0
Due Diligence	0
Purchasing/Escrow	0
For Sale	2
Sell-side Escrow	1

You can combat a bad deal flow by consistently sending out mail. Make a mail schedule and stick to that schedule. If you pause your mail, you will pause your acquisitions which will trickle down and pause your income. In the above situation, you are not acquiring any properties so once you sell what you have, it could be months until you make more money. The whole process takes time. By the time you get it under contract, go through the title, list it for sale, sell it, and go through the title again it can be very time-consuming.

Keep in mind this deal flow strategy is for people who are taking this seriously and want to make a high-income, sustainable business. If you just want to focus on a few deals, your deal flow will never be "healthy" in the traditional sense, but you can still make great money. It just will not be as consistent income. You could make $60,000 one month from a property and then have a couple months without income at all. Keep that in mind when planning your mail and staying consistent.

Case Study: Anthony and Jeff Weiler

Now that you understand the basics of land investing, it's time to look at a real-world example that shows how it can change lives. Jeff and Anthony have been dedicated land investors and came into the industry to have more freedom in their daily lives. With hard work and dedication, Jeff and Anthony were able to make their dreams come true within six months. Let's take a look at their journey:

Background

Anthony and Jeff are a father and son team who live together in California. They have a great relationship and work extremely well together. They got into land investing about eight months ago and have had quite the journey. Anthony works a 9–5 as an analyst and Jeff works in operations.

Introduction to Land Investing

They decided to get into land investing because of the potential upside they saw in it. They were sick of other labor jobs they have had, and they have real estate backgrounds and understood the wealth potential of real estate. They wanted freedom to quit their job and take care of their finances without being stressed.

Obstacles

Anthony currently has $100,000 of student loan debt and has to pay $1,400 a month for this. Finances have been a burden to say the least. On top of this, Anthony has started four different businesses and followed the methods of "gurus" who promised everything and delivered nothing. Some of these businesses included drop shipping and Amazon FBA. Due to these failed businesses, he came into land investing with a lot of doubt—doubt that it was possible and doubt in his ability to be successful. Jeff likewise struggled with some internal doubt about his own abilities in this industry.

Getting Started

Jeff and Anthony sent out their first mailing campaign of three thousand letters in July of 2022. Although they got some good leads and calls from this campaign, they were not able to acquire any properties. This campaign cost them about $2,100. This was the biggest roadblock and obstacle they had to overcome. They'd just spent $2,100 with no results, so now what? The doubts were starting to take over. This was one of the more difficult weeks of their lives, and they knew they had to overcome it if they wanted their dreams of freedom to come true.

Grit

They pushed through it and sent out another campaign of two thousand pieces of mail, which cost them around $1,200. That $1,200 was the breakthrough for them. They were able to acquire three good pieces of land. Below is a breakdown of the three deals they acquired.

Results

Deal 1:	Deal 2:	Deal 3:
Size: 1.6 Acres	Size: 3.9 acres	Size: 1.57 acres
Purchase Price: $30,000	Purchase price: $20,500	Purchase Price: $10,000
Sell Price: $68,000	Sell Price: $47,000	Sell Price: $26,000
Time on Market: 1 Day	Time on Market: 2 Weeks	Time on Market: TBD

Future

After working with deal funders to finance their deals, they took home over $45,000 in profit! This was an extreme confidence booster, and they can now fund over a year's worth of their business and reinvest it into more mail and marketing. They were able to hire their first employee shortly after this to help outsource some of their daily tasks so they can focus on marketing and sales. Their goals are now becoming a reality. Anthony can now breathe without having to worry about his debt. This is only the start to their new chapter.

This success helped them form the confidence and ability to understand that they can do this. Anthony and Jeff have plans to quit their day jobs, hire other family members, and live life with financial security and freedom. If they would have stopped after their first marketing campaign, they would have never known what's right around the corner. Jeff and Anthony both feel less stressed about life and more optimistic about finances and entrepreneurship. I asked Jeff what the best part of this has been and he replied, "I love seeing Anthony smile again."

Wrap Up

Now that you understand some of the advantages of land investing—profitability, simplicity, sustainability, and the freedom it
provides—you now can decide if it is right for you. Understanding
the business model is a critical part of making a big leap into
your investing career. Before making a decision, it is important to
commit to the business and give it your all. As I stated in this chapter, consistency and effort in your mailing schedule is directly cor-
related to your success. In the next chapter, we are going to discuss
what you can expect while you begin the land investing process.

5
WHAT TO EXPECT

Learning Curve

Just like any other business model, there is a big learning curve to land investing. It is very important to understand instant success will not come and there will be major hiccups in your business. You will have times of extreme frustration because you just can't seem to figure something out. This is why it is important to be involved in a community and to keep networking. There are people out there going through the same exact things you will experience during the learning curve; you are not alone. It will feel like you're taking major dips at times, but with continuous education and small steps forward your progress will show over time.

Whether you're joining land investing groups, listening to podcasts, watching YouTube videos, reading blogs, or whatever it may be, it is important to consistently keep this up during your journey. There is a reason why I called it *continuous* education and not just education. By continuing to grow personally and professionally you will stay fulfilled and continue to be forced out of your comfort zone. I am a full believer that information and education, alongside taking action, is one of the most powerful ways of mastering something. You can't do one without the other. You can't educate yourself without taking action, and you can't take action without educating yourself. The most optimal performers are those who do both and do so with a purpose.

Using your resources is the best way to overcome the learning curve. Resources can be anything that help you get from point A to point B. There are free and paid resources everywhere; you just need to find them. When you go through the ups and downs of entrepreneurship it is important to find a way through them, and the best way to find your way through obstacles is through education.

There are three levels of land investors: beginner, intermediate, and expert. Beginners are those who recently started their career and have usually done no deals or maybe just one or two. They are starting their professional education journey, and they are getting ready to take action. Intermediate investors have done typically five to ten deals. They likely are transitioning out of their nine-to-five job or just steadily investing on the side. Then there are the experts. Those are the ones who make high six- and seven-figure incomes. They do it full time and they do it very well. They are dedicated to the business model, have employees, and are scaling their businesses.

It is important to network with all three levels of investors throughout your own investing journey. You may wonder what good would it do to network with someone who is just starting out like you are, but the answer to that is simple: in a year from now, they will be in a completely different spot. They could be experts by then. And they are also going through similar things as you are at the moment, so you can work through obstacles together, jump on calls, etc. So where do you find these investors? At Land Investing Online, we have a free online community, currently in Discord. There are also other land communities on Facebook and on the web. Land investors love to help other land investors, and because there is so much available vacant land out there—roughly nine times the amount of land with houses or structures—there is plenty of business to go around.

Time and Consistency

There are two factors that really matter when analyzing results. The first is time. The saying "the best time to start was ten years ago" is true. Time is your biggest asset. There will never be the perfect time to start, other than now. Time works in your favor because knowledge and experience compounds on itself. One of my favorite marketing "gurus," Alex Hormozi, always says great businesses are built slowly. There is no need to rush and try to sprint for two months and then get burnt out. Consistent and methodical movements are best. I always tell aspiring land investors that it's not about how much time you put in, it's about the consistency. I've seen expert land investors spend fewer than ten hours a week on land investing and be extremely successful because they've put in those ten hours a week over and over and over again without fail. Pauses destroy momentum and they destroy businesses.

I like to call this the six month rule. Put one to two hours a day into something for six months and watch the change and progress you have made. Small steps for six months will get you a tremendous amount of progress. It takes six months to really get a business off the ground; don't get frustrated day to day, but rather think of its long-term progress and goals.

Monthly Expenses and Costs

Now let's jump into the startup cost associated with land investing. If you are purchasing a program or other educational material to follow, then that would be your first expense. But for the sake of this example, we are going to discuss the startup cost not including any education you decide to purchase.

Software

From a software perspective, there is very little financial commitment. We currently use a customer relationship manager (CRM) called Airtable that has a free version. It is a great affordable option if you want to get a CRM set up. But I recommend not worrying about this step until you have deals and calls to actually manage. I recommend starting with Excel, Numbers, or Google Sheets.

The other software we use is The Land Portal. We can see things like slope, water features, wetlands, satellite images, road access. This feature gives us a great sense of the property from aerial footage, and we can usually determine if it is good land. At this time, The Land Portal does offer a free trial, but it is not free long term. Their packages currently run $30 to $60 a month.

Mail and Data

The biggest expenses you will have upfront is mail, discussed in the previous chapter, and data. Data is all of the records that we pull to find the owners of vacant land in the area we are targeting. For example, if we are targeting properties in Hamilton County, Ohio between two and fifty acres, we will pull all the county records on properties that size. We choose to do this through The Land Portal. Each record currently costs six cents. So if Hamilton County, Ohio had 2,000 landowners of lots between two and fifty acres, we would be charged $120.

There are other ways to acquire vacant land that is more cost efficient than mail. Text messaging and cold calling are also common methods. Texting is less expensive, but it is still not free. Right now we use a platform called Launch Control to text, and it costs $500 per month. Admittedly, there are other, more cost-efficient platforms, but Launch Control has been the best I have seen from a user perspective. There are also data costs associated with texting beyond the data that you get about the property itself. You will also need to skip trace to get landowners' phone numbers. Skip tracing is a service where they provide phone numbers for people based on the data we upload. This service typically costs around five to twelve cents per record. On The Land Portal there is currently a five-cent skip tracing option.

Let's dive into an example for your monthly expenses once you have this up and going.

Startup Costs Month 1 (MAIL)
Mail (3000 pieces) = $1,860
Data (3,000) = $180
CRM = Free
The Land Portal = $30 - $60
Total: $2070 - $2100

Startup Costs Month 1 (TEXTING)
Mail = $0
Data (3000 records) = $180
Launch Control (texting platform) = $500
Skip Tracing (.9 x 3000) = $270
The Land Portal = $30 - $60
Total = $980 - $1010

As you see in this example, texting is $1,000 cheaper than sending 3,000 mailers. But what is the cost of responding to all the leads, hiring virtual assistance to help you manage the leads, and getting fewer deals. Like I said, the efficiency of mail trumps texting, but using a combination of both is very effective. Either way, investing is an extremely low overhead business when compared to other businesses. This is a low risk, high reward business model. No loans, employees, rent, overhead, or equipment.

How to Pay for the Land

So let's say you've now sent your mail, obtained leads, and gotten a property under contract to purchase. Let's say the property costs $55,000. The majority of people do not have $55,000 sitting around to fund these deals, so that's where deal funding comes in. You are the manager of the deal, and the deal funder is the "bank." This is a win/win for both the manager and the investor or deal funder. The manager does all the work, finds the deal, sells the property, and everything else in between. The deal funder wires the money and in return you both come up with a profit split which can vary: anything from fifty-fifty to 25/75 percent splits in favor of the deal funder are common. This business model is about building long-term relationships with funders, and cheaper money and more favorable splits will come with trust and experience.

How do you find the right deal funders? Network in your community or land communities. There are plenty of deal funders out there because deal funding is a great way for investors to put their money to work without working themselves. The best part about deal funding for the manager is that they have 0 percent risk, while the deal funder puts out their own money and has the land as collateral.

Another way to gather funds is through traditional banks. You can get loans, a line of credit, or HELOCs. This money is *much* cheaper than deal funding, but it is also riskier. With traditional banks, they report to your direct credit score, and they will attack personal assets if you ever default for any reason. It is also typically a lengthy process to get a loan. I recommend going this route when you have a lot of experience under you to mitigate any issues that might arise. Definitely do not get a bank loan for this business, especially if you don't have deals coming in and out, because these loans typically have monthly payments including principle plus interest. Be careful exploring these options.

Another way to obtain funds, which is one of my favorites, is friends and family. I did much of this while starting my land investing business. My dad, friends, and friends of friends all invested in my deals. We did this on a deal-by-deal basis and would come up with a profit split similar to deal funding. As always when working with friends and family, walk carefully. You don't want any relationships to blow up due to any business-related issues.

And of course, the final way to fund your land deals is through personal money. This probably won't happen until further down your investment journey unless you already have a private fortune ready to invest. Once you are established, you'll be ready to start funding your own deals as well as others' deals.

Wrap Up

My preferred methodology includes a combination of all of these methods. It mitigates risk and keeps everything balanced. My first two years of land investing I made a ton of money on paper. But the problem was that I was reinvesting all of that money back into new land deals and my cash flow was terrible. I just kept buying more and more with 100 percent of my profits. While in theory this is great, it is also good to see the profits and pay yourself for your efforts. By using some deal funding, some personal money, and some friends and family, you can be well balanced and make a killing.

6

CHOOSING A MARKET

Getting into The Weeds

Now that you understand the business model of land investing, we can finally get to the good stuff: investing and executing the deal. Choosing a market is the process of finding the regional location we're going to target, and it is typically the first step of execution in the land investing model. Unlike most other real estate investing models, where you target neighborhoods and zip codes, in land investing we typically target counties. We will examine factors like average days on market, population density, how much land is for sale, and more. The goal of determining these factors is to make sure that we have a good chance of acquiring land, *and* that when we go to sell it, there will be demand for it.

We are going to pull a lot of data and look at lots of numbers, but once you feel good about a county it's time to act on the information. I have seen people get caught up on this area for days. Sometimes the best decision is just making a decision. Don't overthink this part. You will get better at it over time, and you'll realize that it's hard to predict the success of a county without mailing the county. Success is determined more about consistently sending mail, not by what county you choose.

This Can Be Done *Anywhere*

This business model can be done anywhere. Land investors can be highly concentrated in a few areas which can make it competitive. But there is so much land out there you can explore different and newer areas. A good place to start is your backyard. When I got started, I was living in Cincinnati, Ohio. I targeted areas in Ohio, which at the time was unusual for land investors, and I was very successful.

I would stay away from a couple of areas as well: extremely wet areas like South Florida and extremely sloped areas. Investing in mountain regions can be difficult when starting out, too. Check an area by going to Zillow, typing in your county of interest, and clicking "satellite view." You can see the lay of the land from a county-wide perspective. In general, it is important to think outside the box when selecting your counties and avoid what everyone else is doing; that only creates saturated markets.

Choose Two to Three Markets

The first thing we're going to do is choose two to three markets we want to investigate. By market, I mean first regional, then county selections. For example, I could choose South Georgia, Middle Tennessee, and Eastern Oregon as my initial markets. To start, go through the specific areas you are interested in on Zillow. Select "land filter" so you will not see houses or structures. Then click "more" and go to acreage. Filter that by selecting "two to twenty acres" so you do not see anything below two acres or above twenty acres. The last thing to do is click "sold," so you do not see any for sale properties.

Next, scroll around those markets on your map. In general, we want five acres to be retailing for between $20,000 – $60,000 to start. I think that price range gives us the best chance to acquire vacant land. Identify areas where you see this trend because these properties are not too cheap or too expensive—they're just in a great middle ground. If five acres cost $25,000, you know ten acres will be around $40,000 – $50,000 and two acres may be around $15,000. That is a very rough estimate, but we typically do not want to acquire any land cheaper than $15,000 on the retail side. That means our offer will usually be around $5,000 – $7,000 and the work is the same whether it's a $75,000 or $10,000 property. But we don't want five acres to be $150,000 because it's difficult to acquire land that expensive at first, and it also means your larger lots will be $300,000 and up.

Once you find a few counties that meet these criteria, write them down. In general, you can choose a metro area and go two to four counties removed from that metro area. The further you get away from metro areas, the cheaper it can get. Obviously, land in Atlanta, GA is going to be more expensive than land a few counties removed in Crawford County, GA. So choose a few metro areas you're interested in, and then pull information about counties nearby.

County Selection Sheet

Now that you have a few regional markets selected, you'll want to select specific counties. You can do this in a spreadsheet which creates a great visual for us to understand each market and county and helps us predict success. In whatever spreadsheet program you choose, you will want to create multiple tabs. One tab equals one market. For now, you can create one tab for each state. Within each tab you will have columns. The first column is labeled "county." In this column, put five to ten different counties around the market you selected. If you selected Atlanta, GA, put five to ten counties surrounding the Atlanta area. Remember, we want to be two to three counties removed from metro areas to start. The next column with be "population density." Followed by "days on market," then "Zillow for sale land," then "Zillow sold land," and finally "sold to sale ratio." Don't worry about what to put in each column, we will get into filling them out later.

Now that you have five to ten counties in the spreadsheet, you can start pulling data and filling it out. The first area to fill out is population density. To find the population density of any different area, we use a tool called "statistical atlas." You can go directly to this link: https://statisticalatlas.com/United-States/Overview and follow the steps there.

Once you select your state, you'll see the filters on the right side of the page. The filter that says "population" is the one you will want to select. Once you click that make sure to view it by county. Going back to our example around Atlanta, GA, if I were to pull data for Jasper County, GA it is showing "37 per mile," which means there are thirty-seven people per square mile. Generally, we want that number under 150 because it is an easier market when just starting out. Below is a picture of the view when you have the correct filters on. Go through each county and get your population density selected for the five to ten counties you selected.

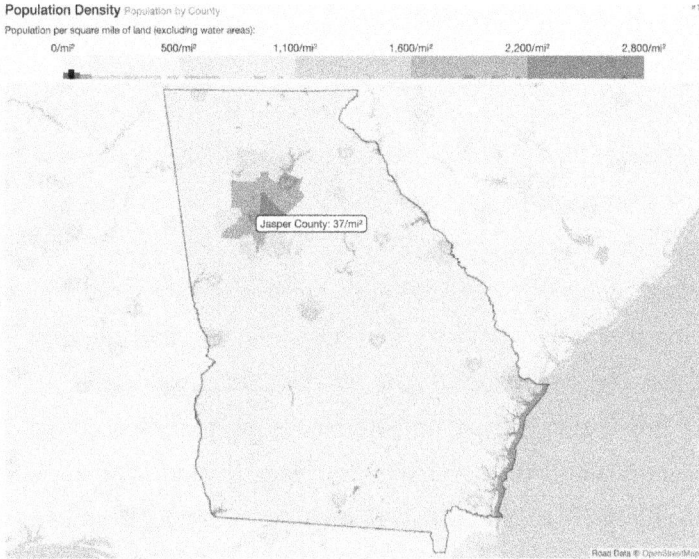

Next you will want to find the "days on market." Days on market is the average days a property is listed for sale before it goes to the "pending" category. This is important because it indicates the desirability of an area and predicts that we can actually sell the land we are buying on the back end. Redfin.com/news/ data-center provides great information and datapoints. Under the section where it says, "Redfin weekly housing market data," scroll over to "median days on market" and select that. After you select median days on market, on the right hand side you will see an area called "region type," auto-selected to show "metro." Change that by selecting "county" instead of "metro." Under that it shows "region name," and from there you will select the counties you listed in your spreadsheet. You will also want to select the two most recent years. One line will show the current year and the other will show the previous year. See the image at the end of this section for how it should look with your filters on. Go to the three most recent data points and average them out. That gives you a ninety-day average. If one month is fifty-five, the next is forty, and the third is thirty-eight, add all three of those together and divide by three to get your average. In the above example, (55+40+38) / 3 = 44. That is the number that goes into your Google Sheet under "days on market." The lower the days on market the quicker properties are selling on average. We want that number under one hundred. Fill this line out for the next five to ten counties in your sheet.

For the last data points, we are going to Zillow to get the "for sale" land listings and the "sold" land listings for quite a few things: gathering data, analyzing pricing, pulling comps, and more. Type in your county in the search bar and you will see the county outline on the map. Now you will need to play with the filters. First, select the home type option, and then select land. Next click "more" and under "days on Zillow," select ninety days so we exclude properties that were listed before that. The next filter to select is under lot size—select two acres and the maximum should be set to one hundred acres. With these filters in the top right you will see X number of results. You can take that number and put it in your spreadsheet. Make sure you have the correct filters on, or your numbers will be inaccurate.

Next, we will want to get the number of sold properties. All you have to do is click where it says for sale and select "sold." Make sure you have the same filters on as you did for the "for sale" properties. You will see the results in the same area as you saw them for the "for sale" listings. Take this information and put it in the Zillow sold column of your spreadsheet.

The last thing we want to analyze is the five acre price. The ideal range is $20,000 – $70,000. Change your filters to two to ten acres and sold in the last twelve months. Do not look at for sale for this part, only sold data. Scroll through and find some sold listings that were around five acres. Four, five, and six acre comps can work for this. We just need to find a ballpark of what fi e acres is worth; that way we know we are targeting areas that are not too cheap or too expensive. We want to avoid areas (at first) that have five acres worth $500,000. You can start going for that market once you're more experienced. If you have a few five acre comps and some four acre comps, average them out. If four acres is worth $40,000, or approximately $10,000 an acre, that would mean five acres would be valued around $50,000. Once you find an estimate of what five acres is worth, put that in the spreadsheet.

Now you should have both the sold and for sale properties columns filled out in your spreadsheet. Use that information to see if the market is saturated with properties for sale, which may make it difficult for you to sell. You will want to divide your Zillow sold column by your Zillow for sale column. See the chart below for an example. The goal is for this number to be around 0.80 or above. Think about it, if the ratio is .40, that means only forty properties sold and one hundred are on the market. Too many properties and not enough demand. During a recession, this number will naturally get lower. We can combat that by buying properties cheaper and undercutting the market. During the COVID era, this ratio was constantly above three, which means three times as many properties were selling than were for sale; it was a seller's market. In both situations it requires us to slightly adjust the business model.

County, St	5 Acre Price	Population Density https://here.com/us-population-density/	Days On Market https://www.realtor.com/research/us-market/	For Sale Zillow (90 days, 2-100 acres)	Sold Zillow (90 days, 2-100 acres)
			Cincinnati, OH		
IDEAL RANGE	$20,000-$70,000	50-150 (people per sq Mile)	14-100 Days	na	na
Hamilton, OH*	$500,000.00	1985	9	10	15
Butler, OH	$130,000.00	800	10	18	17
Warren, OH	$150,000.00	554	11	33	21
Clermont, OH	$115,000.00	445	10	38	28
Brown, OH	$55,000.00	90	18	26	15
Highland, OH	$50,000.00	76	22	15	8
Adams, OH	$42,000.00	47	37	30	14
Clinton, OH	$100,000.00	103	17	22	12
Ross, OH	$70,000.00	112	37	8	16

To bring this all together, you will want to look at all five to ten counties you selected and see which ones best fit your criteria.

Wrap Up

Now that you have all the information you need to select a county, you will have to look at your data and make a decision. There will never be a perfect indicator for what's going to be a homerun county and what's not. The metrics I've outlined have historically done very well for us. But there are no guarantees. However, most importantly, don't get paralysis analysis. You have to make a decision. If none of the counties looks good, keep pulling data for more counties until you find one you like. But remember, it's not foolproof in either direction. We've had success in many counties that did not look good on this report, and we've done deals that were not nearly as profitable as this report would have seemed to indicate. This tool is merely to help you make the best possible estimate given the available data.

7

PRICING AND ANALYTICS

Now that you have your market and county selected you are ready to dive into pricing and analytics for your land investing business. We are going to go into great detail about how to pull your data, scrub your data, pull comps, and then price your offer. This will be one of the more intensive chapters in the book due to the level and amount of information. One thing to note going through this chapter is that pricing is never going to be perfect. There can often be a level of analysis paralysis that occurs, and you'll want to avoid that at all costs. With time and consistency, your pricing will improve greatly.

Pulling Your Data and Scrubbing

Now that you have your county and criteria selected, you will need to pull your data set. This step is easy but can be fairly tedious. Once you master this step yourself, we recommend you outsource it. It is something you can record on a video and have a virtual assistant do very easily. But before you do that, it is important that you really do master it yourself. It is important to your understanding of deals as a whole. If you are less tech savvy and not as familiar with spreadsheets, this could be more challenging at first. Once you do it multiple times, it will become fairly simple.

Signing Up for a Data Source

When sending out mail, you need a way to find the records of whomever owns land in the counties you are targeting. That is where a data source comes in. A data source is a way to extract records of anyone who owns property in a certain area with the filters you choose. For example, you can do a vacant land filter, acreage and size filter, ZIP code filter, and much more. Once we have chosen all of our filters the data source will spit out records of anyone who matches those criteria.

Example Filters:

- County: Hamilton County
- State: OH
- Acreage: Two to Twenty Acres
- Property Type: Vacant Land

In this example, my filters are county, state, acreage, and property type, similar to those we used on Zillow. Once I have those filters in, I can view the results and records in the area. I am going to stick to using The Land Portal for these examples. If you have a real estate background, you may have a different service that you prefer. If you don't have a preference, you can do some research and find a provider to work with. The philosophy and techniques will cross over with slight adjustments across providers.

Pulling Raw Data

Head over to thelandportal.com or your preferred data source to get started. The first thing we need to do is start a new advanced search. Once you have that you can enter the state and county that you selected, along with your acreage range. The Land Portal does not automatically know we are looking for vacant land, so we need to tell it to use the following criteria.

Land Use Filters to Apply

First, you will need to enter in the state and county you desire in your market selection. The Land Portal has a unique AI "Vacant Land" button in the top of your filtered search. This will automatically remove any properties with structures from your dataset. There are a few other filters on The Land Portal that I also recommend using. Filters are ways to clean up your data to get more precise with your marketing, ultimately saving you time and money.

1. **Wetlands** – There is a minimum and maximum field to enter in the percentage of the property you want to allow to be in a wetland. For example, let's say you don't want any property with more than 50 percent wetlands. You would put the minimum value as 0 and the maximum as 50. That is what I typically recommend.

2. **FEMA flood zone** – Similar to the wetlands filter, you can exclude properties in a FEMA flood zone from your data. I like to select any properties under 50 percent.

3. **Landlocked** – This is a yes/no button that can remove any properties that are landlocked. I recommend turning

landlocked filter to no to ensure every property you send mail to will have legal access.

4. **Road frontage** – You have the ability to target specific amounts of road frontage, ensuring that your property is on a legal road, and specifying how much frontage you want. This is specifically powerful if you're targeting subdivisions because the more road frontage you have, the better. I don't recommend using this for standard mailers, but you will want to use it heavily for other future projects.

5. **Others** – Other commonly used filters commonly used on The Land Portal are *out of state, corporate owned, assessed value, delinquent,* and *mortgage amount.* Don't worry about these for now, they are unnecessary for most people at this point. There are a lot of filters you can play with, but people tend to overthink this process. Start with the basics, see what works, and adjust over time.

Choosing Acreages to Send Mail

Since you have your county selected, we now have to figure out what acreages we want to send mail to. Let's use Hamilton County, OH as an example since that's where I'm from. First of all, I do not want to send any mail to small lots. They are very risky, and you can get burned very easily. They are also very difficult to price. I recommend starting at a minimum of two-acre lots, just like we did with the Zillow data.

According to The Land Portal, there are three thousand records of properties between two and twenty acres of raw vacant land in Hamilton County, OH, which is a good mailing list. I recommend that you have between fifteen hundred and four thousand results at a time. If two to twenty acres in Hamilton, Ohio yielded me eight hundred results, I would then expand my search and look at two to fifty acres or two to one hundred acres to get me the fifteen hundred to four thousand addresses I am looking for. Play with the results in The Land Portal and come up with an acreage range that works for you.

Lot Acreage Filter

Once you have all your appropriate filters selected, click "review" to find how many records fit your criteria. The Land Portal offers an option to remove duplicates prior to exporting the data, which will remove any record for someone who owns multiple properties that fit your criteria. I suggest doing that first to save money on mail and data: If somebody has multiple parcels of land, you can negotiate when they call you, and make an offer for the others as well. The Land Portal also offers an option to view all the properties a single landowner owns. When you're finished reviewing the data, click export to download the list into your spreadsheet.

Scrubbing Your List

Scrubbing your list removes any bad records that don't make sense to include. Mail is expensive, so removing entries without zip codes, street addresses, cities, etc., it vital. There are three goals in this process:

1. Remove Duplicates (if not already done when exporting your data from The Land Portal)
2. Remove government agencies (water, electric, fire, police, etc.)
3. Remove any records without mailing zip codes, mailing address, mailing city and mailing state.

If you already removed duplicates prior to exporting, then you don't need to worry about removing them now. If you did not, go ahead and remove any duplicated records that are owned by the same person. You can do this in bulk by carefully going to the column that shows the owner's full name, highlighting that column, and removing duplicates. If you don't have experience with spreadsheets, watch a few how-to videos online, and make sure to cross reference your original data sheet from your data source with the spreadsheet to ensure the columns and rows match up and weren't shifted in the process.

You can do this by selecting "owner full name" and then using Control+F on PC or Command+F on a Mac to search records that contain keywords like water, fire, police, government, county, etc. Then delete each one of those records. Do the same thing for records that are missing their zip codes, addresses, etc. Once this is accomplished, your data set is clean and ready to go.

Reformatting Your Data

Now that the list is scrubbed, move on to reformatting the raw data. Organize the spreadsheet to add specific columns and formulas. If you want to speed this process up, use Landinvestingonline.com to check out available templates. If you choose to make it yourself, follow these steps:

- Add blank columns to your data spreadsheet A – S in this order:
  - » Name
  - » Title
  - » Company
  - » Address
  - » City
  - » State
  - » Zip
  - » Phone
  - » Email
  - » Website
  - » Date
  - » Reference
  - » Offer Price
  - » Closing Date
  - » Offer Price Per Acre (PPA)
  - » Retail Value Profit
  - » PPA Calc Percent (price per acre calculated percentage, which is the percentage we are going to offer for retail value)
  - » Real PPA (real price per acre, meaning it is the retail value per acre)

- Input formulas for columns M and O.
  - » Column M is your Offer Price: (= O2 * T2), which is Offer PPA times Acres
  - » Column O is Offer PPA: (= P2 * Q2), which is PPA Calc percent times Real PPA
  - » Drag the formulas all the way down the columns.

Once you have your pricing formula template ready you will need to copy and paste your data into that template. Paste the scrubbed data starting at column T. The other fields will be populated automatically through those formulas. You will need to fill out columns A – L and drag that down on the spreadsheet so it populates all of the rows for you. Your spreadsheet should look something like the example below. For the closing date, put it at approximately one month after the time you send out the mailer, so it gives the landowner time to review the contract and think about it. The reference number is a unique number for each mailer you send so you can easily look up the field. Below I use HM-OH-1, and it will end with HM-OH-1750 since there are 1750 pieces of data I am sending mail to. HM stands for Hamilton County and OH stands for OH, so every time I get a call I know exactly what property we are discussing. Trust me, when you are sending mail to multiple states and counties, you'll want to make sure to keep the reference numbers unique so you can easily look them up.

Daniel Apke	Owner	We By Land LLC	1412 Winterh: Tampa	FL	3359 513-333-3333 Daniel@Danie Webuyland12	1/10/2023	HM-OH-8
Daniel Apke	Owner	We By Land LLC	1412 Winterh: Tampa	FL	3359 513-333-3333 Daniel@Danie Webuyland12	1/10/2023	HM-OH-9
Daniel Apke	Owner	We By Land LLC	1412 Winterh: Tampa	FL	3359 513-333-3333 Daniel@Danie Webuyland12	1/10/2023	HM-OH-10
Daniel Apke	Owner	We By Land LLC	1412 Winterh: Tampa	FL	3359 513-333-3333 Daniel@Danie Webuyland12	1/10/2023	HM-OH-11
Daniel Apke	Owner	We By Land LLC	1412 Winterh: Tampa	FL	3359 513-333-3333 Daniel@Danie Webuyland12	1/10/2023	HM-OH-12
Daniel Apke	Owner	We By Land LLC	1412 Winterh: Tampa	FL	3359 513-333-3333 Daniel@Danie Webuyland12	1/10/2023	HM-OH-13
Daniel Apke	Owner	We By Land LLC	1412 Winterh: Tampa	FL	3359 513-333-3333 Daniel@Danie Webuyland12	1/10/2023	HM-OH-14
Daniel Apke	Owner	We By Land LLC	1412 Winterh: Tampa	FL	3359 513-333-3333 Daniel@Danie Webuyland12	1/10/2023	HM-OH-15

Pulling Your Comps

In this section, we are going to discuss how to source and use this data to price your mail efficiently. There are many different places you can source your comp data from. Any tool that reliably gets you accurate data and comps can work, but for now we are going to discuss some different methods I have used for pulling comps.

Redfin has a downloadable comps sheet option where you can pull a list of all the comps relative to your filters. Many people in the land-flipping market use this tool regularly. To access it, go to Redfin.com and input your land and acreage filters. Then click "download all" at the bottom of the search form to export the data to your spreadsheet. There are also a wide variety of scraping tools you can use that can pull your filter from Zillow and export it as a spreadsheet. Make sure to set your filters appropriately. If you are targeting two to twenty acres, you will want to see comps of roughly the same acreage range. A two-hundred-acre property is not going to help us price five acres. We need to make sure the data is relevant for what we need.

Another thing to track is the sold date. Generally speaking, the more recent the comp the better. If we have a comp from thirty-five months ago, we know the area has changed significantly and we are less confident in the comp. Whereas, if a property just sold in the last few months, we have more relevant data. If you have a lack of comps in the area, you may have to go back quite a bit to get enough data. That is also okay, but just remember that land appreciates over time.

Prop Stream is another popular source to get your data. This is a subscription-based platform that provides real estate information and comps. You or your virtual assistant can also manually go through all the comps on Zillow and write them down in your spreadsheet. The data you will need to collect include sale price, date of sale, property size, ZIP code, Zillow links, and whatever else you'd like to see there. You should also pull the for sale comps as well, but keep in mind they are often overpriced and will not sell. One thing to keep in mind is that when you are pulling these comps you need to add a column for the time on market. If it was listed 250 days ago it most likely will not sell at that price. If it was listed five days ago you can see how many "saves" and "views" it is getting. That tells you the kind of traction the listing is getting. One general rule to guide you is that if it has more saves than days on the market it is priced to sell.

You can source comps from multiple sources but be sure to remove any duplicates. *And remember to be creative with sourcing your comps.*

Filtering and Analyzing Your Comps

Once you have your list of comps you will want to sort them by acreage from smallest to largest. This helps sort through any outliers and better understand your data. Once you have the data sorted, (and you've already removed the duplicates as previously discussed), you can now move on to removing outliers. Anything that stands out significantly relative to the size of the property needs to be deleted. If you have ten data points that show five acres are selling for around $20,000 and one showing it sold for $100,000, you need to remove it. The data selected should be consistent, any comps that are too high or too low need to be removed.

There are also many properties out there that don't have legal access which destroys the sale price. To eliminate these, you can go into individual listings and read the descriptions and pictures. At times you will see them mention "cannot build on site" or something about the land that speaks to why the comp is an outlier. Another thing you want to do is make sure that the comps on Zillow show the history of the listing. Proper listings will show "listed for sale," "pending sale," and "sold" with an MLS number. But you will also see many comps just show "sold" without the other two stages. Those are typically off-market deals, and we should not use them.

I'd rather have three to five very strong comps than twenty comps that are all over the place.

Now that we've talked about filtering your sold comps, let's talk about the for sale comps. In my opinion, I'd say about 80 percent of land listings are not priced to sell. We have to assess for sale listings more loosely than sold listings. Some people will put their five acres up for $100,000 when all the data might be showing it will sell for $30,000. They are just fishing for offers and hoping to get lucky. When things are this overpriced, they will not sell, period. When things are priced to sell, they generally get multiple saves a day. When something is not priced to sell, they remain on the market for a long time without saves or views.

Once you have removed all your duplicates, outliers, and looked into individual comps, you are now ready to move on to pricing your mail based on this data.

Pricing Your Land
Creating Your Pricing Template

The first thing you want to do after you filter and analyze your comps is break them into segments. As we discussed earlier in this book, land pricing works in segments. The retail value of twenty acres when priced per acre is going to be less than the retail value of five acres when priced per acre. This is because you are bulk-buying land. The more land you have, the lower the price per acre it will be. When analyzing your comps, you need to determine where those price breaks are and figure out what acreage ranges are going to be priced differently. The table below is an example of how your prices could be split.

In our example here, we have two-to-four acre lots that will be priced more per acre than four-to-six, and a four-to-six acre lot will be priced more per acre than six-to-ten acres, and so on. You now have to analyze your data to find out which acreage ranges you want to split the pricing on. This is known as pricing segments. In this example, I segmented them into two-to-four acres, four-to-six acres, six-to-ten acres, ten-to-twenty acres, twenty-to-fifty acres, and fifty-to-one hundred acres. This made sense based on the data I analyzed with those acreage segments all having similar prices per acreages. If you do not have enough data to make a decision, using something similar to the chart below is always a safe bet. In some areas you may see twenty to a hundred acres all have roughly the same price per acre, and you will need to adjust your pricing segments accordingly. The pricing in the chart below was created just for this example, so do not assume it is relevant to any true deal of yours. This is just an example of how the price drops over land size segments.

Acreage Range	Price Per Acre
2 - 4	$10,500
4 - 6	$8,500
6 - 10	$7,900
10 - 20	$7,100
20 - 50	$6,200
50 - 100	$5,750

Choosing Your Pricing

It's now time to calculate the market value for each acreage range you choose to segment out. The goal of this is to not get overwhelmed or discouraged. This is the most difficult part of the process. There will be times when you underprice or overprice an area. It is part of the game. Pricing accurately is a never-ending learning process.

When pricing, the first thing I like to do is take the average of your comps for those segments. In the example above, I would take any comp from two-to-four acres and average them out. I would do the same for four-to-six acres, six-to-ten, ten-to-twenty, twenty-to-fifty, and fifty-to-one hundred. Once you have the averages, I would put them into a chart like the one above where every pricing segment of higher acreages has a lower retail value per acre. If the larger lots have a higher price per acre than the smaller lots, something is wrong with your data, and you need to investigate to see what is going on.

Once you have your average price per acre finalized, you will need to come up with an offer percentage you want to offer them. Below is another example of the offer percentage. What you want to offer them is based on the demand in the area and on average we purchase for around 38 – 50 percent of market value. After closing costs and other fees, we want to always be able to roughly double our pricing. This ensures that we can get funding for the deal and make money after closing costs.

Acreage Range	Price Per Acre	Offer Percent	Offer Price Per Acre
2 - 4	$10,500	38 percent	$3,990
4 - 6	$8,500	42 percent	$3,570
6 - 10	$7,900	42 percent	$3,318
10 - 20	$7,100	44 percent	$3,124
20 - 50	$6,200	45 percent	$2,790
50 - 100	$5,750	47 percent	$2,703

I am often asked, "Why don't you just price at 25 percent and have better margins?" It's because doing so makes it much harder to get deals. I would rather take three to four deals at 45 percent than one deal at 25 percent. It is also much more sustainable. You can offer higher percentages as the deals get bigger because there is more profit to work with.

For something that is worth $10,000, if we offered 47 percent, we would be offering $4,700. After closing cost and fees, we will be at $6,000. There is also some risk in not knowing exactly what it is worth. Then you will have to close on the back end and (potentially) pay out a deal funder as well. The margins can get small in that example. But if we offer less for smaller acreages, we will have more room to wiggle and avoid risk. In contrast, if we offer $100,000 for a $200,000 piece of land, closing costs are only going to be 1 percent of our purchase price versus 10 percent or more of the other example. Also, $100,000 profit is good for future business, so we can be more aggressive with our pricing for higher value properties.

You will need to decide what you want to offer per segment. When analyzing this, you need to make sure there will be enough money in the deal to satisfy the deal funder. With experience, you will master property selection and pricing , and as long as you are providing value to the seller you will get deals. Once you finalize your pricing percentage, you need to enter that into your data. Revisit the section in Chapter 7, "Reformatting Your Data," if you have not done this part yet. Once you enter in your offer percentages and retail value, your data sheet should automatically fill in the rest. So the formula would automatically take: (4.6 acres x 8500 x .42) = Offer Price. Once you have this done and have your file formatted, you can now move on to testing your pricing.

Testing Your Pricing

This is a *very* important step, and you will need to adjust pricing based on your findings. Start by going to your data sheet and choosing five to ten random properties in different areas and sizes. You can go to The Land Portal and type your Assessor's Parcel Number (APN) into the software. We will be using this number throughout the process and it's typically how we look up individual properties. With these five to ten APNs, we want to be able to answer the question, "Will we buy this property for our offer price?" In order to answer that, look at the specific location it is in and the offer price, then pull up Zillow and your comp sheet, and look for nearby sold properties and for sale properties that are very similar to yours. The goal is to make sure you'll be competitive enough, but also that you will not be severely underpriced or overpriced.

Take your time on this step and carefully check the pricing. It will also help you learn more about the area. If your findings show that you are overpriced or underpriced after going through five to ten of these, head back to your pricing template and you can adjust pricing there. Repeat this step until you feel comfortable with your results. There is absolutely nothing wrong with adjusting your pricing. This will help increase your results from your mailer.

Pricing and Sending Your Mail

Now that we have spent time pricing our mail and testing it for accuracy, we are ready to send the mail out. Once you get this step set up, it will be much easier. In this section we are going to go over how to create your template, mail merging, and sending the mail.

Creating the Letter Template

A letter template is the standard offer letter that our potential sellers receive in the mail. Once you have the letter template set up, you can mail merge it with your pricing sheet to auto-populate the fields with the pricing, acreage, seller name, company info, etc. Creating a letter template is a one-time task. To get started, open up Microsoft Word to create a new document. Other programs may work as well, but I've found Word to be the easiest and most functional. If you want to speed this process up, we have pre-made templates available on Landinvestingonline.com. Once you have your mailing template set up, the mailing company you choose will store it in their system so all you need to do is send the formatted pricing sheet.

Below is an example of how you can format your template. The letter is two pages. On the first page, we include a description of what we are looking to do, which is purchase their land. It is an opener to gain the landowner's interest. In the example below, I open it up with "Dear (First Name), Have you considered selling your land in (County), (State)? My company makes cash offers on vacant land all around the country. We specialize in quick and easy cash transactions. You do not have to deal with Realtors, closing costs, or a long waiting period." Wherever it shows parentheses, the mail merge program will automatically populate the info from your pricing sheet for you.

We go on to say, "We can close in as little as ten to fifteen business days." If you have a title company that can close quicker, or takes longer, adjust that accordingly. Then we discuss our offer letter on the second page and how to move forward if they are interested: "On the following page, you will see a purchase agreement with our offer for this land. If you would like to move forward with this offer, you can email us a copy of the signed purchase agreement to (Your Email) or mail the signed purchase agreement to (Your Address). If you have any questions at all or would like to discuss the process, please give us a call at (Your Phone Number)." This is meant to help the potential seller understand the process and what the offer letter is, and what to do with it if they are interested.

Now, let's move onto the second page, which is an actual purchase agreement. This template has worked for us in every state we have worked in so far, but please check current local laws and guidelines to make sure this is legal in the area and market you choose. This is the sales agreement for the seller. The seller will need to fill this out to get the process started. "This offer is for the purchase of real estate in (County, State). The purchase price of (Offer Price) will be paid in full at the time of closing. The real estate we are offering to purchase is (Lot Acres) and the parcel number is (APN Formatted)." Now they have all the information they need. We delivered them the offer price, acres, parcel number, and location. As I mentioned above, we do not manually do this. When we mail merge the documents together, this will go to your pricing sheet and automatically pull the fields over, so you don't need to manually fill in anything that is in the parentheses above.

Next, we get into contingencies. Contingencies are anything that would stop us from buying the property. You can adjust these accordingly, but historically these contingencies have worked very well for us. You want to make sure if the property has a defect, you can get out at any given moment. If a property is 100 percent in a wetlands and flood zone, we cannot buy that property for the amount we offered, therefore we need to cancel the contract. Here are the contingencies we include on our purchase agreement.

This offer is contingent upon the following terms:

1. Buyer's confirmation and acceptance of legal and physical aspects of the property.

2. This offer shall remain open until (Closing Date) and if not accepted by then, the offer shall be rescinded, unless otherwise discussed.

3. Buyer can take title in any entity of their choosing.

4. Buyer will pay for all closings costs.

In the first contingency, this is where we can backout of the physical aspects of the property if it does not meet our expectations. We get into due diligence in the chapter below and there will be many times where you have to cancel the contracts based on findings throughout that process. In the second contingency, we put a closing date to bring urgency. Choose a date about a month after you send the mailer. You want to give them time to think about it and hang it on their fridge. In the third contingency, we explain how we can take title in any entity or business we want. If we use deal funding, the title will often go in their name. This allows us the ability to do that. The fourth contingency explains how we pay all closing costs. This is another incentive for them to sell their property. People hate paying closing costs, so to avoid that issue at the outset, we always pay closing costs on the acquisitions side. After the contingencies, we have the area for the sellers to sign. In addition to signing, we require them to add their name, address, phone, and email.

Take a look at the example below:

(Your Name)
(Your Address)
(Your City), (Your State) (Your zip)

Reference # (Reference)

Dear (First Name)

Have you considered selling your Land in **(County) County, (Situs St)**

My company makes cash offers on vacant land all around the country. We specialize in quick and easy cash transactions. You do not have to deal with realtors, closing costs or a long waiting period.

We can close in as little as **10-15 business days!!**

On the following page, you will see a purchase agreement with our offer for this land. If you would like to move forward with the offer, you can email us a copy of the signed purchase agreement to **(Your email)** or mail in the signed purchase agreement to **(Your address) (Your City), (Your State) (Your Zip).**

If you have any questions at all or would like to discuss the process, please give us a call at **(Your number).**

If you have any other property you are interested in selling, please contact me to discuss further.

Sincerely,

(Your Name)

(Your Name)
(Your Address)
(Your City), (Your State) (Your zip)

Reference #: (Reference)

Sales Contract to Purchase Real Estate

This offer is for the purchase of real estate in **(County) County, (Situs St)**. The purchase price of **(Offer Price)** will be paid in full at the time of closing.

The real estate we are offering to purchase is **(Lot acreage)** acres and its parcel number is **(APN Formatted)**

This offer is contingent upon the following terms:

1. Buyer's confirmation and acceptance of legal and physical aspects of the property
2. This offer shall remain open until **(Closing Date)** and if not accepted by then, the offer shall be rescinded, unless otherwise discussed.
3. Buyer can Take title in any entity of their choosing
4. Buyer will pay for all closings costs

(Your Company)   **Seller**

Buyer Sign: _____   **Owner Name:** _____

                                                    Owner Signature: _____

                                                    Address: _____

                                                    _____

                                                    Phone: _____

                                                    Email: _____

(Your Email)   **(Your Phone)**   **(Your Website)**

Mail Merge

A mail merge is the process of taking your data from your pricing sheet and exporting it into the letter we created in the section above. That is because the fields in the letter template can connect to the fields in the pricing sheet we worked on above. Most mailing services can work with you on this part to guide you through the setup process. YouTube and other resources also have great videos going over this as well.

What we do is take the columns in our pricing template and connect them to the appropriate fields in our letter. For example: in our purchase agreement when we say "This offer is for the purchase of real estate in (County), (State)" we would connect the (County) in the letter to the county column of your pricing spreadsheet template and the (State) to the state column. We need to connect every field from our purchase agreement that has a parenthesis to a specific column in the spreadsheet. Once you have all of them connected, it will take all of your data and merge them to the template filled out for each row individually. Below is what the first page will look like after the mail merge for each of the records you pulled. So if you have three thousand rows after scrubbing your mail list, you will have three thousand two-page letters.

It's important to note that once you set this up, especially with a mail service, be careful not to change the column names, or the data will not pull over correctly. If you do change your spreadsheet, make sure the mail merge is remade with your letter, and that you update your mail service.

(Daniel Apke LLC)
(1412 Winterhaven Ct)
(Tampa), (FL) (33592)

Reference # (HM-OH-3321)

Dear (Mike)

Have you considered selling your Land in **Hamilton County, (OH)**

My company makes cash offers on vacant land all around the country. We specialize in quick and easy cash transactions. You do not have to deal with realtors, closing costs or a long waiting period.

We can close in as little as **10-15 business days!!**

On the following page, you will see a purchase agreement with our offer for this land. If you would like to move forward with the offer, you can email us a copy of the signed purchase agreement to **Daniel@Danielapkeoffical.com** or mail in the signed purchase agreement to **1412 Winterhaven Ct Tampa FL 33592**

If you have any questions at all or would like to discuss the process, please give us a call at **513-333-3333.**

If you have any other property you are interested in selling, please contact me to discuss further.

Sincerely,

Daniel Apke

Sending Your Mail

Now that you have everything ready to go, you are ready to send your first mailer. The mailing company will typically do the mail merge for you and send out all the mail which saves you from licking all those envelopes! Each mailing service has different options and features. Sometimes the mailing companies will try to upsell you, but I advise you to stick to what we know works at first.

Once you have some extra money and a profitable business you can test different mailing options. Rocket Print is a company that many land investors use because they are familiar with how land investing works and from what I have seen, they have been good. I encourage you to talk to multiple companies before getting started to get a feel for everything. Mail prices historically are raised each year: Just two years ago, I remember it being around forty-eight cents. As the price of stamps go up and the price of materials increases, you will see price jumps occasionally. My example of sixty-one cents is just a marker to use but, depending on when you are reading this, it could change.

Alternative Methods of Marketing and Acquisitions

At my company, we do not specialize in alternative methods of marketing simply because the mail and blind offer letter strategy we use has been extremely effective. We have the data from hundreds of thousands of mailings to show that for every piece of mail we send out, we get approximately $6 back in profit. But it's helpful to have a basic understanding on the other options available to you. If you'd rather skip this section and return to the process as I do it, go ahead and turn to "Analyzing Your Results" in Chapter 7.

We have been experimenting and getting some deals through texting recently as well. Texting is a sustainable way to acquire deals, but it is more work and has more operations behind it. I personally like to use both mail and texting simultaneously because you will reach more potential landowners. Whichever way works for you is fine by me.

If you want to learn a bit more about these methods, keep

reading. We are going to dive into some alternative methods of marketing that we have tried in the past, and a few that we have seen others use. The process for each of these options is very similar. The only difference is the method of delivery. Everything you've learned thus far in this book will still be necessary for these alternative methods.

Skip Tracing

We've already covered the basics of skip tracing, but this is especially important if we are texting. We need not just any phone number, but a cell phone number specifically. There are hundreds of skip tracing software programs out there; I encourage you to do your own research on different ones to use if you choose to try these alternative methods.

Texting

Texting is something I have experimented with quite a bit. In general, it is a cheaper financial alternative to mail, but less efficient, so more expensive in terms of time. More conversations are needed with the potential sellers. The goal of a text is to get them on the phone. With a 10 percent texting response rate, you will have to filter through all kinds of texts, which pretty much requires a virtual assistant and management. Mail is still king in my mind, by far.

For texting we currently use two platforms. The first one is called Launch Control. Launch Control is used to send all of our texts and manage our cold leads. The other is The Land Portal which we can also skip trace our leads to get the phone numbers. There are many other programs out there, but I have had the most success with Launch Control. It was also built by attorneys, and they are the most legally-compliant service I could find.

There are two types of texting: cold texts and follow ups. A cold text is sent to someone we have never reached out to by any method. An example text may look like, "Hi Sue, I noticed you owned land in Hamilton County, OH. I am a family-owned business looking to acquire land in the area. I would love to discuss this opportunity." From there, a conversation may start and eventually you build enough trust to get them to accept an offer and you acquire the land. I like to have my data priced before texting so I have a rough estimate of what we can pay. I don't want to have to do due diligence and pricing during every negotiation.

The follow up text is the second method of texting. This is a series of texts that are sent after you send mail. It is nudging the landowner to respond to the blind offer you sent them. An example message would be "Hi ___, did you receive my offer letter on your property in ____ County? I would love to hop on a call to discuss this offer." It is another method to have a touch point with a property owner if they didn't open the mail or have not responded yet.

In general, texting can be a useful way to acquire land. It is just much more upfront work. Whatever method you choose to acquire land can work, but it's all about proper execution.

Neutral Letters

A neutral letter refers to a letter that does not include an offer but is written or presented to a property owner with the intention of gauging their interest in selling their land. There is no dollar amount or agreement attached to the letter. Its purpose is solely to establish initial contact and assess the owner's willingness to sell the property. Neutral letters are something I have done with my company, and I continue to use them in certain situations.

The content typically includes the following:

1. Introduction – The letter usually begins with a friendly introduction explaining the interest in the property and purpose of the letter. This part gives a brief explanation of who you are and a little bit about your company.

2. Expression of interest – Explains the buyer's interest in acquiring properties in the area and explains some general positive aspects about the area.

3. No specific offer – Unlike an offer letter, a neutral letter does not include any specific price or terms for the purchase. It merely expresses a general interest in the property and a desire to discuss the purchase further.

4. Contact information – The letter should include the buyer's contact information which will be very similar to the blind offer template. It will include your email address, phone number, and address so the buyer can get in contact with you.

Neutral letters can be a great way to reach potential sellers. At my company, we are experimenting quite a bit with it. I love to use this technique to attack bigger projects, such as subdividing. The properties we buy for subdivisions are typically larger and more expensive. As you get to more expensive properties, blind offers become harder and harder. Another reason I like neutral letters for large lots is that we are able to offer a higher percentage of what the land is worth for a potential subdivision. Since we are splitting it up, we are often able to pay 60 – 70 percent of the value. Neutral letters work far better to get the conversation going in this situation.

When using these methods of acquisitions it is important to understand two things: The first thing I look at is the seller's motivation. Are they willing to sell for under market value? If the answer is yes, then continue. The second thing I look at is the land. Is this land worth pursuing? I do a quick scan. If the land is worth pursuing, then continue.

Here are some pros and cons of neutral letters:

Pros

- Reach a broader section of those who may have said no to the blind offer.
- Easier to get the conversation going.
- No set price, which means if you're a good negotiator there is a lot of wiggle room since there has been no price mentioned.
- If people didn't respond to your first blind offer, a neutral letter is a great way to get some of the non-responders from your blind offers. When retargeting the same area, this is a great option.

Cons

- More time consuming: Neutral offers are much more time consuming than blind letters. Neutral letters will get a higher response rate, but many of those will want an outrageous amount of money.
- The cost is the same as blind letters but are typically not as effective unless targeting very specific properties where you can pay more for the land than the traditional method.

Overall, I like to use neutral letters to reach those who did not respond to the blind offer, and also to reach owners of bigger properties where I am confident I can negotiate. Big properties can be very difficult to price on the front end which is why neutral letters work so well.

Cold Calling

This is the cheapest option of acquiring properties, but also the most time consuming. Cold calling is the process of skip tracing your data to get phone numbers, then calling the phone numbers to see if they are interested in selling their land. I would still price the data, so you know what you want to offer someone prior to the phone call. Unless you have people working for you or virtual assistants, I do not recommend this method. It can work, but it is extremely time consuming and an incessant grind. You can price mail and send five thousand mailers out in just five hours of work, or you can cold call five thousand people and spend a month trying to connect with them all. At the end of the day, you have to decide what your time is worth.

Emailing

Emailing is a cross between texting and mailing methods. Emailing is unique from texting because you can send attachments with the emails, and you can provide more information. You can structure an email similar to a piece of physical mail, and you can even attach a contract for them to sign and mail or email back to you. You can even get creative and send a DocuSign document for each recipient so they can sign right then and there: no stamps, attachments, or work necessary. Also you can directly provide links to your company's site to build credibility. Just as with every method we've talked about in this chapter, have your records priced and ready to go. After skip tracing your data to get the email addresses, you can use an emailing service to blast out the emails. I have not experimented with emailing as much as texting, but I have heard it can work. If you have a real estate background in house flipping or wholesaling, you may be more aligned with these alternative methods.

Lead Generation Services

A lead generation service is a service that specializes in identifying and providing potential land investment opportunities for investors. They are meant to find potential leads who may be interested in selling their land and handing those leads over to you. Anyone who may be interested in selling their land is a potential "lead."

Here's how lead generation typically works:

1. Data Collection: the service gathers data from various sources such as public records and online databases. They will use filters to narrow down their search and many of

them are flexible so you can tell them where you want to acquire land.

2. Property Evaluation: The service may assess the potential of each property to determine if it aligns with your criteria.

3. Lead Generation: Once properties are identified and evaluated, the service generates leads by providing you contact information and property details of the potential sellers. Typically this is through a list or online portal.

4. Marketing Support: some lead generation services also offer marketing support to help you reach out to potential sellers using any of the methods we've described previously.

5. Tools and Follow-ups: Some lead generation services may also provide tools and systems to track their interactions with leads and manage the process. In this case, we use our CRM program, so it would not be necessary if you are using that.

The downside is they typically are very costly, and most services do not know our business model very well. It is important to not overly commit with a lead gen company, and make sure you can try them out for a few months before committing. You want to see results first. Just because they are providing you the leads does not mean that the leads are always going to be qualified. And you still will need to do your sales and negotiation processes to get it under contract.

Analyzing Your Results

No matter which method of marketing you use, you will need to analyze your results. Marketing without data is impossible to tweak and adjust. You need data on what is working and what is not working. Be sure that you have enough of a sample size out there before you make any conclusions. Send ten thousand mailers before you even consider fully analyzing your results. I know it gets expensive, but it only takes one deal to pay for a whole year of sending mail. Analyzing your results by geographic markets is also important. Try using the following metrics:

1. Leads per mailer (you must define what a lead is for this).

2. Response rate per county.

3. Purchase agreements signed versus how many mailers were sent out.

4. Profit per unit of mail.

For example:
- County: Hamilton County, OH
- Mailers Sent: 4,300
- Leads obtained: 25
- Purchase agreements signed: 4

- Purchased properties: 2
- Total profit: 37,000

Analyzing the Data Above:

- Leads per mailer: 1/172 (meaning one lead per every 172 letters)
- Profit per unit of mail $8 per piece of mail ($37,000 profit divided by 4300 units of mail)
- Purchase agreements versus mailers sent: 1/1075 (One purchase agreement for every 1,075 sent)

Above is just a very basic example of things you can analyze. I encourage you to carefully analyze results and come up with your own metrics for your unique situation and approach to land investing.

Wrap Up

The most important thing to remember with pricing and analytics is to be consistent and to be patient. Some of the tasks we discussed in this chapter will take you two hours when you first start out, but just ten minutes once you get the hang of it. Remember, focus on filtering your comps. There are too many bad land comps to take them all seriously. One of the biggest mistakes beginners make is putting too much weight on bad comps. Whether it's overpriced, bad land, or an old comp, you have to adjust accordingly. Learning to properly assess comps is one of the most important things you can do to be successful in land investing. Pricing is difficult; don't give up, and remember it gets easier over time.

Case Study: Matt Pamfilis
Background:

Matt is originally from Baltimore, Maryland and is twenty-four years old. Right after Matt graduated from the University of Tampa in Entrepreneurship, he started his real estate journey. Matt currently does land investing full time while still wholesaling houses. He originally got into wholesaling because of the low barriers to entry and he saw it on Instagram. After running into difficulties with wholesaling, he decided to intern for a successful wholesaler who showed him the ropes. After that internship he went back to wholesaling himself and wholesaled thirty-nine infill lots in 2022. For those who don't know, an infill lot is a smaller parcel in a subdivision, typically anywhere between a quarter acre to two acres. The building market started to dry up and Matt knew he needed to pivot immediately, which got him to investigate land investing.

Intro to Land Investing

Matt had already heard of subdividing land and owner financing. He'd looked at some YouTube videos and eventually found the land investing space. Matt immediately went down the land investing rabbit hole and would constantly listen to podcasts, watch videos, and read articles. It took about three months of researching before Matt pulled the trigger and dove in full force.

Obstacles

Since Matt came from the wholesaling world, he had to retrain his brain for our business model. Coming from a world of cold calling and texting, he had never sent mail before. Sending mail is easy, but the pricing aspect can be difficult. Matt used a few people in the community to get help with pricing, and eventually felt good enough to send out his first mailing. Matt's first mailer got some leads back but no results. He then had to overcome the obstacle of having a "dud" mailer and move on to his next batch. Another challenge Matt faced was the delay between sending the mail and obtaining the lead. He was used to near instant responses from his wholesaling days, but mail takes one to three weeks for the leads to even receive it. Additionally, the price of mail was a challenge. But Matt knew this would work and knew it came from within him to make it happen. The business model is proven, so why couldn't he do it? That mindset helped him get through the tough times.

Getting Started

Matt got started in November of 2022. He sent out his first mailing campaign shortly after that. He sent his first mailer to a small county in Maryland where he got no results. His next mailer led to three deals. He ended up buying his first property in January and two more shortly after that, all in Tennessee, and he was able to arrange deal funding for all three of them. Since then, Matt has negotiated three more deals in South Carolina, totaling six deals in about six months. Matt's deals sold for less than what he was anticipating in Hickman County, TN, but he still made decent margins. Within eight months of starting, Matt was able to net over $250,000 of profit before deal funding splits. After funding, he will net well over six-figures in the first eight months of starting!

Determination:

Matt knew that this business model works, and he knew he could do it full time and make great income. He came in extremely aggressive and determined to make it work. Since Matt had the experience from wholesaling, he knew that the execution was the part he needed to work on. Fortunately for Matt, he was able to get three deals off his second county to support the proof of concept. Matt didn't question the business model's ability and believed 100 percent he would make it happen.

Results:

- **Hickman county**
  - » Property 1:
    - Buy $11,000
    - Sell $20,000
    - Profit before funding: $9,000

  - » Property 2:
    - Buy $20,000
    - Sell $34,000
    - Profit before funding: $14,000

  - » Property 3:
    - Buy $20,000
    - Sell 41,500
    - Profit before deal funding: $21,500

- **Chester county**
  - » Property 1:
    - Buy $18,000
    - Sell $85,000
    - Profit before deal funding: $67,000

» Property 2:
- Buy $32,500
- Sell $75,000
- Profit before deal funding: $42,500

» Property 3:
- Buy 52,000
- List 189,000 (current list price)
- Projected Profit before deal funding: $137,000

Future

Matt wants to make $100,000 a month from this business and then start exploring different niches like subdivisions. He currently has one full-time virtual assistant but will hire more in the future when needed. His goal is to keep this business very lean, outsource much of the internal work, and focus on the bigger picture tasks himself. His goal is to build this up then buy rental properties. Matt has received a tremendous amount of freedom from land investing. Within eight months of starting, Matt was able to obtain the six deals above, which will net him over $250,000 before funding splits. After splits, he was able to make well over six figures in just his first eight months.

8

ACQUISITIONS

Getting Prepared for Phone Calls

Getting prepared for leads to come in is an important part of the business. About two weeks after you send your mailer, you will start getting calls. It is important to have a system in place for when those come in to organize your leads. We use a software called Airtable for our lead management, but there are plenty of other options. You can start by using a spreadsheet to organize them.

The first thing you'll need is a phone system. You can use your own phone to start if you must, but eventually you will want a unique number for your business. I have used a phone service called OpenPhone in the past, which has done well for us and our members at Land Investing Online. To start, get a phone number that is unique to the markets you selected. If you are in the south, get a southern number, but you don't need one for every city or area you are in. For example, if you are doing business in Georgia,

Tennessee, and Alabama, one area code would work just fine for all three states, but it is important to choose an option that allows you to text. When acquiring properties I like to be able to text about updates or even receive the purchase agreement over text.

The other communication you will need is an email. I recommend opening a Gmail account dedicated to the business. The Google suite of programs is very affordable, and you can scale with it. If you do not want to pay anything, just open a standard Gmail account dedicated to the business. We get a lot of email responses from our mailers, so this is an important feature to have set up in advance.

Social Proof Helps

In general, the more social proof the better. By social proof, I mean having a website, Facebook page, maybe LinkedIn, or other social media platforms. Anything to prove that you are a legitimate business. At first, I wouldn't worry too much about having a website set up if that is daunting to you, but down the road you will definitely want one. A website with testimonials, an "about us" page, etc., will all help, especially as you look to expand. The more personal you can be, the better off you are. Local landowners prefer to sell to local family-based businesses rather than big conglomerates, so be personable on your social platform. Make a human connection with the community.

When I first started, I did not create a website, but I did have a Facebook page. That worked well and a lot of people looked at it. You can put the link to it in your mailer, so people go to your Facebook URL instead of a website. Even if you have a website, creating a Facebook page is still important, and make sure to post on it every so often to fill it out and make it look more legitimate. Post your phone number and information there as well. This may sound basic, but sometimes I see pages that are missing the most basic things. It is important to create your social proof to help comfort potential sellers and show them they're in the right place.

Occasionally you will get a call from a seller, especially when you're new, who thinks you may be trying to scam them. Usually they are interested in selling but are skeptical. One of the main ways I overcome this is through local title companies. Refer them to a local title company and let them know everything is going through a title firm to represent both sides. If you've used a title company before, that's even better because you have a relationship with them. Assure the seller that all closings go through a legitimate legal process and have them call and review the title company. This has been one of the most effective ways to overcome skeptical sellers in my experience.

Just remember, it is important to be personal on all of your social media platforms. People buy and sell to other people, and they want a personal touch. Make your company look as solid and professional as possible.

Inbound Calls and Sales Tips

Now that you have your systems in place, we can now discuss inbound calls and sales tips. The goal of every inbound call you take from a potential seller is to get the purchase agreement signed. That needs to be your goal and that is what drives business. Getting the purchase agreement can involve several different factors. Sometimes people call in and are ready to sell on the spot and just want to confirm a few details. Those are the best and easiest leads.

Some will want to negotiate; those are some of the hardest calls, but they can still bring you a lot of money. The others will simply call you to tell you to f*ck off. Don't be intimated, it's part of the process. Just move on.

Let's go deeper into negotiation because it can bring you a lot of money once you get it right. It is important to always ask the right questions and gather information. You can better understand the seller's motives and, ultimately, that can help you negotiate. The more facts you have on the seller the better. It is important to gather these facts along the way. Let's say a seller calls you back about a five-acre property that you offered $25,000 for. The seller is asking for $10,000 more, so $35,000 total. The question you want to know is why they are asking for more and what makes them think that's a fair offer. Some people will tell you they bought it for $35,000 and don't want to lose money. Those people are less likely to move from that number in my experience. If someone calls in and wants $100,000 for that property, that's typically the worst type of lead and they are not going to sell at a reasonable price. The majority of people who call and ask for $35,000 in this example are people who just want to negotiate and will meet somewhere in the middle. Often, we will hold our ground at the original offer price if we think we priced it well and you'd be surprised how many of them still sell. But most of the time, we will meet somewhere in the middle depending on how that negotiation goes. They won't come to my number, and I won't go all the way to theirs.

During negotiations it is important to find out if there are any other decision makers involved in the process. Some other questions are the following:

- How long have you owned the property?
- Do you live in the area?
- Have you been to the property?
- When is the last time you've been to the property?
- Why did you buy the property originally?

Now we can use some of those questions to help us in the negotiations. If they don't live in the area, we can help them liquidate it fast, and we also know out-of-state buyers are often very hot leads for us. If they have owned it for twenty years and have never been to the property, it's usually from an inheritance and they have no skin in the game. They are likely just sick of paying taxes on it. Over time, you will better understand how these questions relate to selling their land, but you should go through these questions with your potential sellers first, regardless. Remember, if they want to sell and don't want to negotiate, there is no need to do this piece. Skip it and just get the purchase agreement sent to you.

The last thing to note about negotiation involves building rapport. Sellers always want to sell to other people they are comfortable with, so be personable and build a relationship with the seller. Don't be a robot—ask some questions and have fun. If you're ever competing with another land investor in a negotiation, the seller will go with the buyer they have a rapport with, all things being equal in the offers.

An easy way to improve your sales skills is to use a friend who is in sales to help mentor you. Find someone who is great at it, have them listen to your calls, and then evaluate them with you. Even if they don't know the business, they know sales, and most sales are very similar: you find the customer's needs, articulate how you can help their needs, and close the deal.

For some of you who don't have any sales experience, contact calls can be intimidating at first. But I assure you, with experience and practice you can become a great salesperson. I like to say there are two ways to turn a D+ salesperson to a B+. The first way is to outsource it or find a partner who excels in sales. The second way is to transform your own skills by practicing over and over.

During these calls it is important to stay confident and understand your value. Some people go in thinking that we are ripping these landowners off. That is not the case. There is value in things other than money, and that is the gray area where we operate. If someone needs money and doesn't want any hassle, that is the value we provide them. Cash offers can also be more attractive than financed offers. Time is a resource you can't discount either. Fast sales at lower prices can often beat higher prices in slow sales. Understanding your value is important to helping you feel confident during negotiations. You have to know what you bring to the table beyond the financial incentive. This business model would not work long-term if we were not providing value to the sellers.

Finally, you have to ask for the purchase agreement. I like to use the line, "Are you ready to move forward with our offer?" Based on how they react, you can make adjustments from there. Many times they will say yes, and you just need to get them to sign and send the purchase agreement. If they have a hesitation, address their concerns. Many times they need to check with family to see about selling. See if you can loop their family members in on a call. Always try to address any issues or hesitations before getting off the call. Finally, make sure to ask when they plan to send in the purchase agreement. It gives them a timeframe for submission and a conscious commitment. It is important to not act desperate during that conversation. Simply ask, "When can we expect the purchase agreement back from you so I can keep an eye out for it?"

Getting the Property Under Contract

There are four main ways you can receive the purchase agreement. Once they sign their side and are ready to move forward, it is time for you to tell them how to send it. The first method is the seller sending you a picture of the agreement by text. This is probably the most common and quickest way. Another option is by faxing it, which is surprisingly still used in the land space and especially with our demographics. The third way is through snail mail, which is the slowest and least common. You want to avoid that due to extra delays, but occasionally elderly sellers will go that route. Lastly, they can sign through DocuSign, Adobe Sign, or any e-signature company. This is a great way to go if you negotiate a change in the price because you can easily edit it on an electronic document. If they do not have access to email, you can have them cross off the sales price on the letter, write in the new price, and initial the change. I have never had a title company say no to this.

If there is more than one seller who owns the property, you will need all owners to sign an agreement. They can sign the same one or you can make more than one copy and send them individually. Essentially the title company just needs to make sure all parties are willing to sell.

The goal for you is to make it as easy on the seller as possible. That is why we provide all of these ways of sending the signed contract and doing business. You want to be flexible in every aspect of business on the acquisition side because the sellers are liquidating their land to us for a below-market value price because of ease. It is important to provide as much value to that end as possible. Lastly, don't get desperate. Sellers see desperation and are not attracted to it. It's a sign of weakness and an easy trap to fall into with your first few deals. If they don't send their contract right away, don't panic. Once you get more deals under your belt, you will naturally come off more knowledgeable and confident.

Double Closings and Wholesaling

When flipping a property the traditional way, you typically have to purchase it at 50 percent of market value or less to have a sustainable business. But this provides a tremendous amount of value for the seller as we act on speed and convenience. If the seller won't budge and wants 60 percent or 70 percent of market value, there are other options. Before considering these options, remember that the deal needs to make sense from both sides. You want to make sure the seller has motivation to sell, and the property is desirable and good land. If both of those things check out, and they simply want a little more money than what you initially offered and can fund yourself, consider the following option:

Double closing, a.k.a. a back-to-back closing, is a strategy used to buy and sell a property on the same day, or within a short timeframe. This is usually deployed when the deal is too risky or too expensive to buy with your own money or a deal funder. It allows you to mitigate some risk while still making some money. Instead of buying the property in two weeks like we state on our purchase agreement, we will have to go to the seller and negotiate ninety to 120 days to find a buyer. For this you will need to either use another template or add a contingency to the current purchase agreement stating the buyer will allow ninety days to market the property. After that, you will need a new signed agreement so you can begin marketing the property to find a buyer. This process gives us the ability to market a property that we don't own and find a buyer. For example, let's say I was under contract with Megan L. to buy her property for $60,000. Megan agreed to give me 120 days to market the property because she wanted more money than I could give her. I know this property is worth $90,000 to $100,000, so now that I have the new agreements signed, I'll go look for buyers and list it at $90,000. Once I find a buyer for $90,000, I set up a time to close the property for the future buyer and seller on the same day. Some title companies can use the funds coming from the buyer to give to the seller, so no money will ever be taken out of my pocket. Otherwise, money is only out of my pocket for a short time. Talk to your title company to discuss best practices and what needs to be done. During closing, I will net the $90,000 - $60,000 = $30,000 (minus closing costs, if any). I have the ability to take the deal that I would have potentially thrown out and make up to $30,000. It is fairly straightforward and will get easier with time and experience.

When considering these options it's important to comply with local regulations on what you can and cannot do while listing a property that you don't own. You often will have trouble getting it on the MLS, so you will have to list it on alternative sites such as Facebook Marketplace, Land.com, and Craigslist. Talk to a local professional or attorney before starting this to make sure you are being legally compliant.

Double closing may sound great, but it can be a risky

transaction. A lot more can go wrong. Since you don't own the property, you have to manage both sides instead of just selling the property. You have to find a buyer while keeping the seller happy and hoping they don't back out. Due to managing both sides at once, it can be much more difficult to scale up, but I do recommend it, especially for beginners who are just trying to get some deals done.

It's very important to be transparent and honest with the seller. "I can't make this work to buy it myself like I'd love to. But what I can do is get you your money in ninety days, if you allow me to market the property and get a buyer lined up. I can get you over a revised purchase agreement to state this and get the ball rolling to find you a buyer."

It is important to note that double closings can involve some additional cost, such as transaction fees and holding costs, because the investor briefly owns the property between the two closings. Additionally some states might have specific regulations and requirements related to double closings. Do your research and comply with the local laws when using this strategy.

Mitigating Risk

One thing to keep in mind while moving forward on deals is how you can use your professional community and deal funding partners. You can have your deals reviewed by other land investors who are very experienced. This is something even experienced land investors do. It never hurts to get another pair of eyes on your transaction. There are a couple ways to do this.

1. Network in the land community and build relationships. They can help review your deals and you can help review theirs. At first you may think you may not provide any value, but soon enough you will have the experience.

2. We host live calls to review deals and so do plenty of other people. Bring your deals to live calls in different land communities.

3. If you plan on using deal funding, then use your deal funder to help you analyze a deal. Many times they are great at underwriting deals and can provide you with some quick feedback.

This will help mitigate any risk. This is one of the primary reasons my company has never lost money on a land deal, out of the thousands we have done. We simply compile other opinions to come up with a decision. Land investors love helping each other—we're all in it to learn and grow together, so take advantage of it!

Case Study: Shelby Wengreen

Background:

Shelby is originally from Ogden, Utah and went to college at Utah State University. Prior to graduation in 2020, Shelby worked in a corporate setting doing marketing. Shelby had no real estate experience or entrepreneurship experience. Her goal was to quit her job in five years in order to be able to be a stay-at-home mom and work as an entrepreneur on her own schedule. Shelby originally came into this by herself but ended up partnering with her brother-in-law throughout the journey. Shelby was determined to make it work and would do anything to take her dreams into reality.

Intro to Land Investing

Shelby was currently looking into rental properties and other types of real estate. She quickly realized a lot of the traditional methods are not built for that type of cash flow that she would need to get out of her job. Since her goal was to quit her job in five years, she knew she needed something with heavy cashflow to replace her nine-to-five job. She even started renting out her driveway to people on the side to raise additional capital to invest. Then Shelby heard about land investing. She originally heard of land investing through her uncle who did well buying and selling land in his early days. Her uncle loved the idea and said he would invest in the properties if she were to get some. Once that happened, Shelby went through over fifty podcasts to learn more about the land investing space. She fell in love with the vision of becoming a full-time land investor.

Obstacles

Shelby had very early success and bought a property in the first four weeks of getting started. That property ended up selling in a day and she made $17,600 (gross): bought for $15,000 and sold for $32,600. Her brother-in-law, Chase, was the one who funded this deal for her because he saw the potential income and decided to partner with her. Little did they know it would take them another six months to get another deal. Shelby felt the pressure of Chase joining in as a partner and really wanted to make it work for both of them. Together, they ended up investing more time, energy, honest self-assessment without excuses, and money into the land investing business and made it work. Shelby attributes the six-month deal pause to not knowing how to price and analyze comps correctly. Shelby was also a part of an accountability group that helped her push through it. The result was that three months after that six month pause Shelby would be able to quit her job and accomplish her lifelong dream of being a stay-at-home mom.

Determination:

Shelby knew that this business model would work, but they had to stick with it. Since they had a deal fairly early, they were confident it would work and started looking for ways to better their business. Shelby and Chase were some of the most consistent land investors I have seen, and they stayed optimistic through the whole journey. They knew what their goals were, and they were going to find a way there.

Results:

- **Haralson county**
  - » Property 1:
    - Buy: $9,000
    - Sell: $19,200
    - Profit: $10,200
  - » Property 2:
    - Buy: $10,800
    - Sell: $20,000
    - Profit: $9,200

- **Madison county**
  - » Property 1
    - Buy: $88,000
    - Sell: $180,000
    - Profit: $92,000
  - » Property 2
    - Buy: $15,000
    - Sell: $25,000
    - Profit before deal funding: $10,000

- **Bourbon county**
  - » Property 1:
    - Buy: $165,000
    - Sell: $438,000
    - Profit before deal funding: $273,000

- **Laurens county**
  - » Property 1
    - Buy: $6,500
    - Sell: $13,000
    - Profit: $6,500

- **Putnam county**
  - » Property 1:
    - Buy: $4,000
    - Sell: $14,000
    - Profit: $10,000

- **Crawford county**
  - » Property 1
    - Buy: $6,000
    - Sell: $14,000
    - Profit: $8,000

Shelby has two other properties on the market that have not closed at this time.

Future

Shelby's goal is to make $1 million in gross profit in her second year in the business. She and her partner are currently undecided whether they want to scale a full business or just operate alone.

Wrap Up

Acquisitions are a huge part of our business. It is where the process starts, and it drives all the revenue. If you are not a natural salesperson, work on it, listen to your recorded calls, and get a sales mentor to help you. You can transform yourself from a D+ salesman to a B+ by practice and repetition. Remember, be as easy as possible when dealing with sellers. Do as much work for them as you can and make their life as easy as you can. Don't forget to ask for the purchase agreement when they've agreed to sell. If you have both good land and a good deal, but the seller wants a little more money, consider double closing. Use the land sales community and build relationships to get your deals reviewed and mitigate any risk before you purchase the property.

9

DUE DILIGENCE

The Property Is Under Contract, Now What?

Once you obtain the purchase agreement there are several things that need to be done. The very first thing I always do is a quick property check. I use thelandportal.com to visually look at the land. On The Land Portal, I look at the shape, slope, location, and I check if there are any features on the property, like access points or other features such as ponds, creeks, or structures. The goal of this step in the process is to see if your land is worth pursuing. Sometimes you will get a purchase agreement back from landlocked properties, properties in wetlands that cannot be built upon, or extremely sloped properties, and more. We have to do a complete due diligence examination on each and every property. Analyzing land from The Land Portal takes time and patience. At first you may not be able to tell the difference between a great piece of land from a bad piece of land. Once you analyze several properties and start to see trends, it will get easier. When in doubt, move the process to due diligence—you don't want to lose any good pieces of land, especially at first when you don't know what you're looking at, but we'll get into those details later in this chapter.

The next thing I like to do is a quick price check. You want to make sure you're not overpriced. We typically want to see properties priced from 35 to 60 percent of market value. We will get more into how to evaluate pricing later on. Like I mentioned earlier in the book, analyzing land can be one of the trickiest parts of land investing, especially because of the comps.

Next, we should start thinking about money. Ideally, you want to have deal funders or other financing lined up, or at least have started the conversation. Historically, if you have a good deal, you will find good funding fairly quickly. Building those long-term relationships is crucial so you can secure financing for all your deals. The better the deal, the easier it is to get money. I would personally start this process before even getting a purchase agreement, just to start building rapport early and making it easy in the end. Deal funders get a lot of funding opportunities, and we want to work with people who work hard and come prepared. The more work you do upfront before sending us a property the better. Once you get your due diligence finalized, you should send the report to the deal funder. If you are buying the property yourself, then you have nothing to do at this step.

Before moving on, know that things sometimes happen with a deal, and occasionally deals will fall through due to a variety of reasons. Here are some examples of why deals occasionally fall through.

1. Title issues: The seller needs to go through probate, or does not actually own the property, or it's a broken title.

2. Inaccurate pricing: Pricing is too high. If this happens, you typically go back to the seller and negotiate a lower price if need be.

3. Extreme defects: This could mean a steep slope, water, or location in a flood zone.

4. Extreme restrictions: This might be strict HOAs, covenants, and other restrictions.

5. Access: Occasionally you will get back properties with no legal access. Even if there is physical access, that does not mean there is a legal access.

The fewer the restrictions and defects, the better. We like to buy and sell great land. The more defects and restrictions you have on a property, the fewer buyers there are who will be willing to buy it. Say you start off with a hundred potential buyers with zero restrictions or defects. Let's say you find a restriction like mobile homes are not allowed. Then you find another defect like half the property is in a wetland. Now your list of interested buyers has gone from one hundred to thirty people. That is the thinking you have to employ during the acquisition process.

Planning and Zoning

Next you will want to contact the planning and zoning department. Give them your parcel ID and ask them about the property's zoning and what can and cannot be done on the property. There is a planning and zoning person in almost every county, but some counties may be harder to work with than others. Since your target counties are rural and small, there is often only one person in the county in charge of a department, and they will have other responsibilities or jobs, too. If you want to find out the specific zoning for your property, you can go online and find that county's zoning policies. In general, you want to be able to do as much as possible with the land you are purchasing. The fewer zoning restrictions the better. You also want to find out what the setbacks are—setbacks are how far off the road and off the sides you can build. Here are a few restrictions to look out for.

- Single wide mobile homes or mini homes
- Double wide mobile homes
- Minimum square footage for building
- RVs/campers

Although there are many more restrictions out there, those are some of the ones you will see most often. One thing I always look for when evaluating properties is if mobile homes are allowed, in both the nearby town and on the property. Mobile homes are very desirable in America, and although it may not seem like it, many people want to be able to put a mobile home on a property. With the increase in housing needs and the cost of living, there is a need for more affordable housing. That being said, mobile home popularity changes state by state, and I start to get very concerned with restrictions when there are too many vacant lots around. Depending on the situation, that can mean people don't want to deal with the restrictions, which means you may have a small buying pool.

The last thing you will want to do is check if it is within city limits. Even though the county may have very few or no restrictions, the city will have its own set of restrictions. A lot of cities restrict mobile homes or other types of buildings more than county regulations do. If the property is outside city limits, you can skip this step, but it is always important to find out. Remember, the more information you have upfront, the easier it will be to sell.

Health Department

Next, you will want to talk to the health department. This is a very simple and straightforward part of due diligence. You want to see if there has ever been a perc test filed with the county. A perc test is short for "percolation test," and it is a soil test conducted to evaluate the absorption rate of soil for the purpose of installing a septic system. A septic system is a sewage system for a property that does not have a connection to public sewage. Remember, we are looking at properties in rural America, and outside of most cities there is no public sewage. Septic systems are very common in rural America. You will constantly hear this term throughout your land investing career.

The perc test determines how quickly water can penetrate the soil, which indicates the soil's ability to handle wastewater from a septic system. A soil scientist digs a hole in the ground and fills the hole with water to test the soils' ability to drain the water. Before building a structure, people need to have a perc test done and filed with the county health department. A failed perc test on a smaller property of two acres or less is a big deterrent, and I would not pursue that property. When you have a property of four acres and above, there is so much room to install a septic tank, that a lack of a perc test isn't something that we typically worry about as much. If you have a fifty-acre property, the chance of it not passing the test somewhere on the property is highly unlikely. But if there is ever a failed perc test on a property, I would not buy it. Future buyers are not going to want a property that they may not be able to build a home on, and you can't build a home on a property that cannot have a sewage system. There are alternative septic solutions if you do have a failed perc, but it gets very costly, and you typically need engineers to design it to fit your property. I have had properties I'd already purchased fail a perc test during the selling process because the future buyers wanted one before closing. This is always a bad thing, but we agreed to sell them the property $15,000 under the agreed upon price to account for the cost of installing an alternative septic system. So do your due diligence and call the health department to see if anything has ever been filed with your property.

Electric

Next you will want to do a quick electric check. Your buyer will want to be able to put electricity into any buildings. Typically, if you have houses around the area, you will have electricity in the area you can hook up to. But I've seen people run into trouble when they have no neighbors within a mile or more, which means they may have issues hooking up to power. Call the local electric company and see if there is electricity in the area. To find out which local electric company runs the area, you can contact the county and simply ask them. This is probably the easiest and most straightforward step in the due diligence process.

Deeds and Documents

Next, get the most recent deed(s) from the county in order to complete your due diligence. Depending on your county, this can be an annoying part of the process and not as easy as it sounds. Call the county clerk's office and give them your parcel ID number to look up. They should be able to send you a deed. If they are giving you a hard time, I have hired people off Craigslist to go in person to get the deeds. In the deed, you can make sure the owner is the actual owner on the deed, and they have the right to sell it. You can also find out about any deed restrictions.

Another document you will want is an old survey or a plateau map. Not every property will have this available, but if the area has ever been split up or subdivided, the deed will sometimes refer to a survey or plateau map. This will show you the outline of your property and confirm all the details like road access, size, and other aspects. This is especially important if you are concerned about legal access or easement. An easement is legal access to a property that is not on a road. Essentially, it's the right to travel through other properties to get to your property. If you have a landlocked property that supposedly has an easement, it is vital to get a survey or plateau map that shows this legal access. Selling land without legal access confirmed is very difficult. You cannot build on a lot that does not have legal access, so it is important to confirm a legal easement if your property is not on a road. See the below image as an example. The red outline shows the property. There is clearly a dirt road going to the property cutting through the property in front. Although there is physically a road, we need to make sure that is legal access before buying this property. You will run across properties occasionally with physical access but not legal access. If you do not have a legal easement, that will often kill the deal. Another option you have is getting an easement from a neighbor, which usually requires a little money and time. These are all things you need to deal with when flipping land.

Water

Water is another utility we will want to check for before purchasing a property. In rural America, it is common to have wells on properties that do not have public water. Call the county and see if they have public water available at your property. More times than not, there will not be public water. But that's okay. We just need all of this information upfront so that when we go to sell the property, we can market it accordingly and answer any buyer's questions easily. The cons of well water is it costs more money upfront to install. The benefit of it is that you don't have a water bill, although the pump costs a little bit in electrical power.

HOAs

You will want to check and confirm your land is not in an HOA. If it is in an HOA, you will want to find out the desirability of that specific HOA. I have had much more difficulty selling properties in HOAs than not. HOAs are essentially another layer of "government" with more rules. People, in general, don't want rules on what they can and cannot do with their properties.

If your property is in an HOA, the first thing you want to see is if there are empty lots nearby. If 75 percent of the lots are empty, that is a sign the demand for those parcels is not high. If 90 percent or more of the properties are filled, you know there is a demand to be there. Find out the HOA restrictions and all of the HOA fees during this step of due diligence. If you don't know if the property is in an HOA, read the legal description. Many times the legal description on The Land Portal will say something like: "Lot 12 of Barkley Estates." Then you can Google the Barkley Estates subdivision in Hamilton County, OH and get more information on it. Another way to find out is by asking the seller if it's in an HOA and if they have any information on it. That is honestly probably the easiest way to find out. But as we know, not all sellers have even been to the land or know anything about it, so we always want to confirm what a potential seller says.

Drone

Before purchasing your land, you will want a personal inspection. Whether that's a drone or a Realtor, it is important to get boots on the ground before purchasing. We will discuss using a Realtor later in this chapter, but my company gets drone footage before every single purchase. We always ask for specific views of the property such as:

- Arial footage of the whole property with an outline of our parcel.
- A ground picture showing the access from the road looking into the land.
- Ground photos of the roads both ways.
- Arial footage of the back of the property.
- Ground photos inside the property if possible.

By having these views of the land, we can help mitigate most risks and get answers to any questions we have. By using these photos in conjunction with The Land Portal map features, we can be sure we are buying a good property. Occasionally, drone photos will show things like extreme slope off the road that The Land Portal did not identify.

If you have an attribute you want to show off, such as a pond, lake, river frontage, creek, waterfall, or anything else that would catch a buyer's eye, you'll want to tell the drone pilot to include those shots. We can use those for marketing to show we have beautiful photos of the property that attract future landowners.

Slope

Slope is a very important subject that can make or break a deal. Slope can be tricky, but there are two main ways we can evaluate land from a map perspective. The first way is to look at The Land Portal contour lines. Contour lines show the slope of a property and can be odd to look at initially. They are essentially lines going through the map that show it either going up or down. They can be ten-foot, twenty-foot, forty-foot, or eighty-foot lines, meaning between each line there is either ten, twenty, forty, or eighty feet of elevation. The closer the lines are together the more sloped it is. See the following picture of two properties slope we can review.

Property A

Property A is forty acres in Oklahoma. The road is directly to the east of the property, so we know they will need to build a driveway or have access off that road. These are only ten-foot lines. If these were twenty-foot lines, the slope would be much more dramatic. As you see in the center of the property the line spaces out and it becomes flat. The slope of this property goes from 890 feet to 950 feet uphill from the east, then falls back down from 950 feet to 890 feet on the left side of the picture. So it slopes up from the road, flattens out, then slopes back down. In general, this land looks buildable, but there is one concern about how steep the slope is off the road. Any time a property goes steep uphill or downhill from the road, it can make it difficult to build.

The Land Portal also offers a measurement tool to measure a slope. In Property A's case, you would measure from the right of the property to the center and find out the distance. Then measure from the road to the center where it flattens out at about 550 feet. Now I can take the total elevation gained, which is seventy feet (seven lines at ten feet each equal seventy feet) and divide it by the total distance of 550 feet. That gives me a 12.7 percent slope. A 10 – 15 percent slope is usually okay as long as there is a buildable flat area. Anything above 20 percent is extreme slope. In this case, since we have a flat spot at the top and the nearby neighbors are on similar slope, I would be okay with this. I think this property has huge potential.

Property B

Property B is what a fairly flat parcel looks like. Lines are spaced far apart, and the front is very flat. Matter fact, there is a small circle on the top of this image near the property border. Whenever there is a circle like that or larger, that means that is a flat area with no slope. This is a beautiful property without slope concerns and the top part of the parcel would be a perfect building site with nice land behind your home.

Another way to check slope is through Google Earth. You can go to the street view of a property and see what the slope looks like from the ground. Another option is to use the evaluation tool on The Land Portal where you can save your map and download the KML file, which is a file format used by Google Earth. Once you download the KML file it will look very similar to your property on The Land Portal. As you have seen in the image below, this property appears to be flat for the first 250 feet, then it slopes up. You can use the ruler then click "path" and click "show elevation profile" to get this view. You always want to confirm that the slope on The Land Portal is similar to the slope on Google Earth. You can also get a ground view from here and get a little better sense of what is going on with the property. Between using The Land Portal, Google Earth, and drone photos, you will mitigate most risks. We are currently in development for a new AI tool to evaluate and understand slope on a property which should make it much easier to understand.

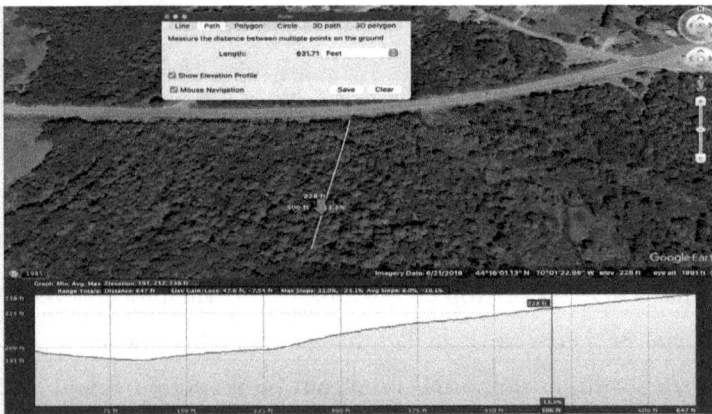

Wetlands and FEMA

A wetland is an area characterized by the presence of water, either permanently or seasonally. It is a unique ecosystem that forms a transition zone between terrestrial and aquatic environments. Wetlands can be found in various locations all over the country. In general, you do not want to buy properties covered in a wetland, but you can have larger properties be partially in a wetland. Just like slope, we want to make sure there are buildable and dry spots as well. Wetlands are a defect for properties. In general, you cannot build in a wetland, and the ground is wet or soft so it limits what can be done. Along with that, there are legal restrictions that do not allow you to build on or change wetlands.

Now let's discuss a FEMA flood zone. FEMA, or the Federal Emergency Management Agency, designates floodplains—areas that are susceptible to flooding during periods of heavy rain, storms, or other natural events—based on detailed analyses and maps that indicate the likelihood of flooding in particular areas. FEMA puts out a flood zone map, also known as a flood insurance rate map. If a property is in a FEMA flood zone, it does not mean it is a wetland, but generally wetlands are also FEMA flood zones. If your property is in a FEMA flood zone, the first thing you want to do is determine if it's a wetland. If so, then that is very alarming. If it's only a flood zone, the first thing to check is the neighbors. Are other people in the same flood zone building on those lots? If your land is partially in a flood zone, and there are buildable parts of the land not in a flood zone, then that is usually okay. You just want to make sure the lot is buildable. I have bought and sold many properties in FEMA flood zones. I currently live in St. Petersburg, FL and half the city is built in a FEMA flood zone. That being said, if there are no other parcels in the flood zone with homes under construction, stay away. Either way, building in a FEMA flood zone requires an extra layer of insurance and is still considered a defect. Not all future buyers avoid flood zones, so it is important to talk to the county on what can and cannot be done in your specific flood zone and what the history of flooding has been.

In general, wetlands are worse than FEMA flood zones, because it is actively a wetland. FEMA flood zones can be dry for a hundred years and then a storm comes in and floods the area.

Below is a picture of a property I bought that was partially in a FEMA flood zone. The highlighted blue area is the flood zone. I was not a bit concerned about this because there was so much land that was not in the flood zone, and it was a beautiful property that could be built on elsewhere.

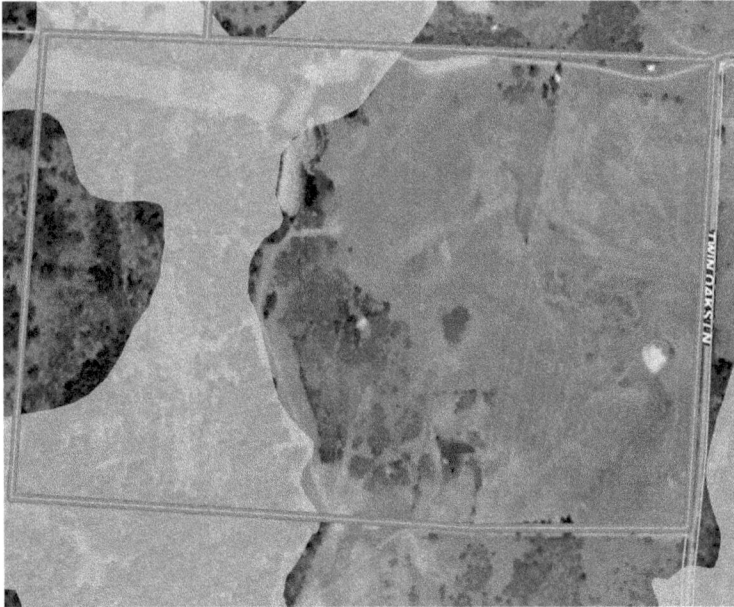

Evaluating Comps

You'll have to forgive me if some of this repetitive of previous sections, however evaluating comps is extremely important and it probably bears repeating some of the information in this case. Evaluating comps and analyzing prices for land can be one of the trickiest parts of this business model, especially in areas where the comps are scarce and spread out. The same obstacles we face when pricing we will face when evaluating land. You may see one comp going for $25,000 an acre and another sold for $10,000. In this section, we are going to address the challenges and come up with solutions on how to comp your land.

Similar to pricing, it's about quality of comps rather than quantity. I'd rather take one or two good comps rather than twenty comps bunched together. The reason behind that is because there are so many bad land comps that are public record and never listed on the MLS. In general, you want to find similar comps to what you're evaluating. If you have a five-acre parcel in the Southwest, you'll want to find a similarly sized property, in a similar area with similar features. That can be the tricky part; sometimes there are not many comps that fit what we are analyzing.

When evaluating these comps I want to see the speed of the market as well. In Zillow if you're looking at sold comps, you can scroll down on the comp and see "price history." You want to make sure the listing was a "real" listing, because they sometimes just report public records, which give us inaccurate comps. To find out if it was a real listing, you should see the date it was posted and the sold price. In the example below, we can see on April 24, 2023, this 23.5 acre property was listed for $49,900. It also has an MLS ID # as well. On April 28, you see it went contingent, and then on June 15, 2023, it closed and "sold" for $40,000. They took a $9,900 below listing price offer in four days after it was listed for sale. You know this is a real listing because it has the MLS ID # and shows the transition from "for sale" to "contingent" to "sold."

23.5 Acres

S Bogus Holw, Union City, TN 38261

○ **Sold: $40,000** | Sold on 06/15/23 | Zestimate®: None ?

Est. refi payment: $227/mo Ⓢ **Refinance your loan**

Home value   Owner tools   Home details   Neighborhood details

Price history

Date	Event	Price
6/15/2023	Sold	$40,000 -19.8%
Source: RRAR #44067 Report		
4/28/2023	Contingent	$49,900
Source: RRAR #RRA44067 Report		
4/24/2023	Listed for sale	$49,900 -15.4%
Source: RRAR #RRA44067 Report		

Now let's look at another example of a "fake" comp in the same area which showed that 4.4 acres sold for $70,000. Upon going and inspecting the price history, I notice it is a "public record," which means we don't know where this came from, and it is not monitored like the MLS is. To be clear, we cannot trust public records. If you see a comp like this, discard it. This applies to pricing as well; we cannot take public records into account when pricing. They are inaccurate and can skew your data.

4.4 Acres

Stafford Store Rd, Greenfield, TN 38230

Sold: $70,000   Sold on 11/14/22   Zestimate®: None ?

Est. refi payment: $397/mo Ⓢ Refinance your loan

Home value   Owner tools   Home details   Neighborhood details

Price history

Date	Event	Price
11/14/2022	Sold	$70,000 +536.4%

Source: Public Record Report

Another way to evaluate a piece of land is to use a Realtor. Using a Realtor on the front end (before purchasing the land) can be a bit tricky since you don't own it yet. You can call around and find good Realtors, which we will go into during the marketing chapter of this book. I like to utilize Realtors before I purchase when I have a great relationship with a Realtor from other listings. It is tough to get a Realtor to do something for you before you even own the land without an existing relationship.

Final Price Approval

During your final price approval process, you will review all of your current due diligence records on the land along with the price and all the information we collected above. The goal of this is to package everything we know about the land and make a decision on if we're buying it or not. Your first property is always the hardest, and it is important not to get emotionally connected to it. During this period, we want to keep all emotions out and make a good business decision. Once you have multiple deals in the pipeline, that gets easier. But until you get your first deal you can get emotionally attached to properties. Create a due diligence checklist.

While making a decision, it is important to factor in closing costs. Depending on your state, closing costs are anywhere from $800 – $3,000. In the Northeast, closing costs can be especially expensive. If you are purchasing the land without deal funding, you can work with tighter margins since you won't be splitting profits. If the margins are too tight, deal funders will say no, but if it's good land and in a good area, then the reward will often outweigh the risk, if it's your own money.

Another thing to do is send this property to your deal funder to evaluate. If it's an experienced land investor, that can really help point you in the right direction. Utilize your deal funders to help make decisions but remember if they say no, that does not mean it's a bad deal. Sometimes they have financial constraints, don't invest in certain areas, don't evaluate land appropriately, or they just make a mistake. You'll want to use the deal funders knowledge as another due diligence data point, not a complete solution.

If it is too expensive and you cannot buy it due to that, you can always call the seller and negotiate down. These are extremely uncomfortable conversations at first, but they are very crucial to master for long-term success. Occasionally, we will accidentally overprice counties and just cannot pay that much. That is okay. That's why our contract says we have to physically inspect the property before closing. We can call back if need be and try to get it for less. I have negotiated down about 20 – 30 percent of potential deals from the original price due to defects, slope, overpricing, and more. Getting comfortable with those conversations is important.

I like to mentally grade a lot's price, property, and location. of these on a A, B, C, D, F scale and help weigh them against each other. First, let's start with price. How is our price relative to the market? Do I have an incredible price on this piece of land knowing that I need to double my money? If you have a property under contract for $30,000 that will resell for $100,000, that is an A price. If you have a $60,000 property under contract that's worth $100,000 that's more like a C+ price.

Next let's take a look at the property. By property, I mean how is the actual land. Are there negative attributes? Is it free of any defects such as extreme slope, wetlands, etc.? Does it have good road frontage? Are mobile homes allowed and are there few land restrictions? Is the shape of the property ideal? By answering those questions you can come up with a grading for your property. If it's a perfect square property on a main road with a nice pond on it, no wetlands, and no defects, that would be an A property.

Next let's talk about the location. Does it appear to be in an attractive area that will quickly sell? How are the other properties in the area selling that are priced correctly? If you're in a great, desirable area then you will have an A location. There are areas of the country that are much slower than others and you will naturally have to wait for your property to sell even if its priced accordingly. Now that you can grade your price, property, and location accordingly, we can talk about the risk associated with it. Let's say for example you have the following property

Price: A
Property: C-
Location: A

Since the price and location are an A, that is probably a risk I would take even though the property is a C-. Here is another example:

Price: C
Property: A
Location: A

Although the price isn't great, since the property and location are so good this is another one that I would do. Since the location and property are great, the risk goes way down. I love buying properties like this. You're in a location where a stunning property will turn fast and/or appreciate. These are deals I want since there is little risk.

Once you have your due diligence checklist, your comps, and you feel good about the land, it is now time to decide and send it to title. This is exciting part of the process, and we make money when we buy properties because of the price we get them for. Remember, if you need help, reach out to mentors or someone who can help. If you have a business partner, you both should be involved in this part of the process.

Wrap Up

It is important to use your resources such as mentors, land investing groups, Realtors, and the available comps. It is all of these elements together that make the decision, not one specific data point. You can use a Realtor if you have a good relationship with them, or you can try to sell them on your future value of using them to list properties and maybe then they will do some upfront work for you. There will be times where you have to negotiate down. Getting comfortable with those tough conversations early is extremely crucial. You will land more deals by negotiating down, and you will be surprised how many people will sell at a lower price if needed. Finally, getting your funding situated is a big part of this business. This business model works so well because there is so much available deal funding out there. Build early relationships with your deal funders to ensure smooth transactions.

10

TITLE AND ESCROW

Identifying Local Title Companies

Title companies play a big part of the land investing business model. Having good, reliable, and fast title companies is crucial. I have had experiences where we have been burned and lost deals because of title companies. It is important not to overlook this step. Spend time looking for reliable title companies. Treat this as a long-term, business-to-business relationship that will grow in the future.

The first thing you want to do is call around. We typically use local title companies, but there are national ones as well. In rural America, it is important to use local title companies because the documents can be difficult to acquire, and having a local company who has more access to more local information can be helpful. I typically call three to five title companies for every market I have. Obviously, if you have already done deals in this market, you can use the title company you've used in the past if they've done well. Here are some common questions you'll want to ask:

- What are the fees associated with a real estate closing, including document and recording fees?
- How long does a typical search take, including time for an attorney to review and approve?
- Will I be assigned a specific transaction coordinator/paralegal who will provide quick responses to me?
- As a remote land investment company, we require remote closings. Do you allow remote closings, and can we use our own notary?
- How do you insure a client against wire fraud?
- Do you hire outside title abstractors, or do you have in-house abstractors?
- Are there fees associated with a transaction we need to cancel after the title search is complete?
- Are lower rates available for volume?

These questions are standard interview questions we use when identifying the right title companies to work with. By getting answers to these questions ahead of time, you can now hold the title company accountable for them. If they said they can close properties in two to three weeks and four weeks go by, you can refer to the initial question you asked them to hold them accountable. It helps to set expectations upfront rather than trying to work from behind. When choosing a title company, it is much less about money and more about speed and reliability. Since our average profit per deal is $23,000, we can afford to spend a couple hundred extra dollars if needed to get a good, reliable title company.

You will also want title insurance for every property you buy. Title insurance protects you from financial losses due to defects in the title of the property. When you purchase real estate, you acquire title, which is the legal right to own the property. However, there can be hidden issues or claims on the title that may arise, but title insurance and a title search can protect you from them. It is something we do for every single deal no matter what, and it helps protect us and the future buyer. The future buyer will want insurance, so we need to make sure it is insurable before we buy.

Here are a few things that title insurance can protect you from:

- Errors in public records and/or recording of deeds, mortgages, liens, or other legal documents.
- Unknown liens on the property and claims against the property that may affect your ownership rights such as unpaid taxes, mortgages, or easements.
- Fraud or forgery: instances where someone fraudulently or improperly transfers the property or forges a signature on a document related to the title.
- Undisclosed heirs or missing heirs: this is a common one. Sometimes somebody else owns the property in the family, and someone tries to sell without that person.
- Invalid or improperly executed documents: issues arising from documents that are not legally valid.

Your title insurance policy will protect you from any of the above, and it is never worth the risk of not being protected just to save a few hundred bucks.

Once you feel good about your title company, you can now send the property to them. I usually email the purchase agreement and business documents and information to them. If you have your employer identification number (EIN) number, Limited Liability Company (LLC) documents, or any other business docs, you can send them to the title company. Different title companies require and ask for different documents. So you can send them the purchase agreement and wait for their response to see what is needed. If you are closing in your own name, you will obviously not need business documents sent to them. Once you send them the documents, it is now in their hands and your job is to follow up and make sure everything is on track.

Speed, Speed, Speed

Since the value we provide to sellers is quick and easy cash closings, we want to make sure they really are quick and easy. This helps ensure you will have a happy seller at the end of the transaction, and it lowers the odds of you losing the deal. It's a game of speed; you want to close your property as quick as possible and the quicker you close, the quicker you'll have your pay day when you sell it. It is not often you lose sellers during title, but it can occasionally happen. You can prevent this by speed and using reliable title companies. That is why we asked up front how long they take to close the transaction with title insurance. We have had to fire title companies in the middle of a transaction simply because of delays and unresponsiveness. I understand things occasionally come up, like broken title or extra work they will need to do, but you should have smooth transactions about 80 percent of the time.

Follow Up and Stay on Top

It is important to follow up with both the seller and the title company. The worst thing you can do is get the purchase agreement from the seller and four weeks goes by with no word. At Apke Land, I like to follow up with title companies every week or so to make sure it's still on track to close when expected. Then you can take your updates from the title company and pass them along to the seller. Be transparent with all parties. If there is a delay, let the seller know what's going on. I always like to ensure the seller I want to close this deal as fast as possible, and I'm upset about the delays as well. Great land investors do a great job of keeping the sellers happy and keeping the transactions moving.

If something happens in the title process that causes a delay or a pause, you want to make sure to keep it moving forward. You do not want to have a transaction paused for a week before making a decision. For example, the title company may require you to get a survey that will cost $2,000 and take four extra weeks. The first thing you need to do is make a decision then pass it along to the seller and explain the reasoning behind it. Here is an example conversation:

Me: Hi, Mr. Votto, I wanted to provide you with an update regarding the sale of your land. Unfortunately title ran into an issue with the boundaries, and they will not insure the current land without doing a survey. Unfortunately, I am not able to purchase land that I cannot get title insurance on. I still really want to move forward with this transaction, so I talked to the surveyor, and they said it will take about four to six weeks to complete. I just wanted to have this conversation with you upfront to let you know there will be some additional time needed that I did not plan for.

Mr. Votto: How much does it cost? I'm not happy about this delay. I was hoping we could close next week like originally stated.

Me: I understand, and I'm disappointed as well. I really was looking forward to the closing next week. Every title company will require this survey before purchasing so unfortunately, we cannot just switch title companies. Are you okay with us going ahead and ordering the survey of your land? We will cover 100 percent of the cost survey, and we don't need anything else from you but a little patience due to the delay.

Mr. Votto: That's unfortunate, but I guess there is nothing we can do. I am okay with it. I'll let my wife know since we were planning on getting the money next week, but I appreciate you letting us know.

That is a very standard conversation. The key takeaway from this conversation is:

1. I updated him with all the information I had without letting it sit any longer before making a decision

2. I was very upfront about the delay and gave him extra time in case the surveyors took longer than expected. I

always like to under promise and over deliver; it creates better customer satisfaction.

3. The more updates the better, but don't overdo it and call every single day. Typically I see members of the Land Investing Online community doing the opposite and having too little communication.

Mobile Notary Versus In Person

The title company is going to need to know if the seller is closing in person or remotely. You, as the land investor, will always close remotely, which is why we asked those questions while vetting the different title companies. Sellers are always welcome to close in person, but the problem with that, as we mentioned earlier, is our sellers are often not in the area. That being said, we have had sellers drive ten hours to close in person, so it is always worth giving them the option. You will need to call the seller and ask what they prefer. If they close remotely, either you or the title company will organize a notary to go to their house or other location as requested.

There is one problem that occasionally rises when closing remotely—skepticism. Since they are signing documents before getting the check, this can create the seller to fear a scam. If they do this, it is important to walk them through the process and potentially connect them with the attorney at the title company or a representative. You can also let them know the only way they can get paid on the spot is by showing up in person. Even with in-person closings, the seller signs before receiving the check.

For your side of the closing, the title company will email you documents to be signed and notarized. Often, they will not require us to notarize, but that depends on the state and title company. I hired a mobile notary off 123notary.com and she comes to my house once or twice a week. I pay her $80 per closing and she prints and sends the documents via UPS or FedEx. I always make sure she has a shipping label to send the documents back to the title company. Sometimes the title company will provide this, sometimes not. You always have to check. You can also go to a local UPS store; they almost always notarize for money. Or you can go to a local bank; my Chase Bank requires an appointment but does it for free.

Reviewing Final Documents

Reviewing your final closing docs is a very important process. On the buy side this will typically be more straightforward since we're purchasing in cash and no Realtor is involved. You'll want to make sure to look at the final Department of Housing and Urban Development (HUD) Loan, which will tell you the amount going to the seller and coming out of your pocket. You will see a line called "due from seller." That is the total amount you owe. That is the amount for you or your deal funder to wire to the bank. If you are using funding, you will need to send that to the investor. They typically will review the HUD as well. You'll want to make sure all the numbers on the HUD document make sense because you will owe more money than is going to the seller—for title insurance, recording fees, document shipping, etc. Below you will see a sample HUD loan that we closed on. The seller received $90,000 and the title company received $1,216 for the other fees.

| Seller | | | | Buyer | |
Debit	Credit			Debit	Credit
		Financial Consideration			
	90,000.00	Sale Price of Property		90,000.00	
		Loan Amount			
		Escrow/Title Charges			
		Abstract/Title Search Fee to Guardian Title, LLC		250.00	
		Post/Shipping - Buyer to Guardian Title, LLC		30.00	
		Settlement/Closing Fee - Buyer to Guardian Title, LLC		275.00	
		Settlement/Closing Fee - Seller to Guardian Title, LLC		275.00	
		Owner's Title Insurance to Guardian Title, LLC Coverage: $90,000.00 Premium: $360.00 Version: ALTA Owners Policy (2021)		360.00	
		Recording Charges			
		Recording Fees to Marshall County Chancery Court Clerk		26.00	
	90,000.00	**Subtotals**		91,216.00	
		Balance Due FROM Buyer			91,216.00
90,000.00		**Balance Due TO Seller**			
90,000.00	90,000.00	**TOTALS**		91,216.00	91,216.00

Below is a list of the things that I check before closing the property.

- Property Details: Ensure accuracy for the listed acreage, address, buyer and seller name and addresses.
- Fiancial Details: Ensure accuracy for sales price and earnest money, application escrow and recording fees, Realtor commission if applicable, prorated amounts for taxes, and closing cost distribution per the sales agreement.
- Title Insurance Review: Check the property detail and legal description and that the proposed insured is properly named including exceptions and requirements. You want to always make sure the property is insured without expectations and requirements. If you have questions on this part, always ask the title company. Read through the policy and look for requirements and exceptions, then address them with your title company. They are usually happy to help on this part.

Once everything looks good on the HUD and closing statements, you are ready to close on the property and wire funds.

Congratulations!

Congratulations, after the seller and you sign, you now own the property. But before celebrating, let's get it listed. In the next chapter, we will discuss marketing your land for sale. This is a crucial part of creating a profitable land investing business. Since we've officially closed the property and now own it, we can now list it wherever. Since a lot of our marketing was done upfront with drone photos, we want to make sure to have plans to list it while closing, and get it posted within twenty-four hours or so of the closing, if possible. If you are using a Realtor, it may take a bit more time, but remember time equals money.

Purchasing your land is a big step in the business. You understand how the process works now, and it gets *much* easier over time. What may have seemed like a hassle initially will be easier every time. Stick with it because the profit is well worth any hassles.

Wrap Up

To wrap up title and escrow remember that identifying the right upfront title company is crucial. It is better to do upfront work and ask the right questions than come from behind because you chose a bad title company. Speed is the essence of this business model, so make sure you're informing your sellers about any updates you receive from the title company. Always keep the transaction moving forward; do not allow for any pauses. Finally, reviewing final documents and title commitments is the last step before closing. Read through those boring title commitments to make sure there are no requirements and exceptions. Title companies are all similar, so when you have questions use the Land Investing Online community or contact the title company with questions.

11

MARKETING YOUR LAND FOR SALE AND ALTERNATIVE WAYS

Acquiring the land is a big part of the game, but selling the land is the next mission. You should put an equal amount of focus on selling your properties as you did for acquiring them. In a hot market it is easier to lean away from the disposition side. Disposition is the act of selling, and I will use that term throughout this chapter. The reason you can fall away from this in hot markets is because it is so easy to sell. When the market balances back out, you will need to be prepared to put extra focus in this area. In general, in hot markets it is easier to sell and harder to acquire. In cold markets it is easier to acquire because people need money, and harder to sell because people are tighter with their money. In general, marketing your property in the correct areas with the correct strategy is vital for your long term success. In this chapter we are going to go over different strategies to help you best optimize your profits.

There are two ways to sell your property: you can flip it, or you can seller-finance the deal. Seller financing is where you act as the bank and provide a loan to the buyer and in return get a down payment, and typically a hefty (8 – 12 percent) interest rate throughout the duration. These are typically terms much shorter than your traditional mortgage. I often see five- or six-year seller financing options. We will discuss seller-financing in greater detail in later chapters, but in general, my firm likes to sell on the market the traditional way, not using seller financing. For this strategy, the buyer either uses cash or gets a loan elsewhere. There are also banks that lend on land that they can use. It doesn't necessarily matter how they get the money, but they are responsible for getting it.

The more impressions and views a posting gets, the more likelihood the property will sell so we always want to get it listed in as many places as possible. In order to do that you need to not only be listed in the right areas, but also have the right price, pictures, and descriptions. The combination of those three things makes the posting attractive. If you have great pictures and the property is too expensive, the property won't sell, and vice versa, if you have a great price and a horrible posting, it will take longer to sell.

In general, marketing your property correctly helps make more money and speeds the cycle of the deal. If you are marketing properly, your business financial situation, including your deal funder's situation, will be in a much better place. Deal funders love speed; they want to take that money back and put it into more properties. When listing your properties it is important to have your funder in mind, especially at first. Good relationships are built around good deals. Like I mentioned earlier, always under promise and over deliver. Making your deal funders happy will open up their wallets more in the future. You may only have one deal right now, but in the future, you will have five to ten deals at any given time and need much more money and need it fast.

Where to Post

Now let's get into where to post your properties. MLS, Land.com and Facebook Marketplace are the three main posting sources I like to use to ensure we are getting a lot of eyes on the property. Since you are posting all the same property across multiple plat-forms, just create one good posting with pictures and then copy and paste. The first one we will discuss is the MLS which connects to fifty-plus sites, including Zillow, Redfin, Realtor.com, and more. It also connects to the local agents' MLS feed, so Realtors representing clients will see the posting. The MLS is the number one place you want to be listed.

There are two ways to post on the MLS. Using a Realtor is the first and simplest way to get your property posted, but the problem with that is it's not always beneficial for you to use. The other method to getting your land posted on the MLS is through someone called a flat rate broker. A flat rate broker is a person or business who takes a fixed fee to get the listing posted on the MLS. Their only job is to get it posted so it goes on all the MLS sites. They will also forward you any leads that come through. The problem with the MLS flat rate brokers is that they can be outdated, janky, and a pain. If you plan on using a Realtor, don't worry about this step, but it helps to know about it for when you do sell the property yourself and don't want to use a Realtor. Below are some flat rate broker sites I have seen members of the LIO community use.

- Homecoin
- List With Freedom
- Broker Direct MLS

Like anything, these brokers can be rather difficult to work with at first, but as you gain experience it gets easier. Many land investors use flat rate services, so it is always good to ask around for opinions and recommendations.

Another place to list is Land.com, which is the parent company of Land Watch, Lands of America, and Land and Farm. If you are using a Realtor, before signing with them, make sure they are a member of the Land.com network. Land.com has serious buyers, and although you don't get as many leads, the ones that do come in are serious. It is expensive but worth it to list with them. They have different packages to choose from, and they will put you in touch with a sales rep. Another advantage of using a Realtor is that you don't need to list it in these places as long as they are doing their job.

Facebook (FB) Marketplace is one of the best places to list land, especially for properties under $50,000. You will be shocked how many properties you sell here. What you need to do is get in the different local land groups within Facebook so you can list them on those groups as well. Facebook leads are not as good in general, but the leads are such high quantity that buyers do come eventually. We will discuss how to handle these leads shortly but having copy and pasted answers is ideal. The best thing about Facebook Marketplace is it is 100 percent free. Like I mentioned earlier, the more exposure the better, so it is crucial we list everywhere. FB Marketplace will not be utilized by Realtors, so what we do is answer the basic questions and forward the leads to the Realtor or put their phone number in as the contact if you have their permission to list their phone number in public.

Craigslist is another free resource and the last one we will discuss here. Historically it has been decent, but not great, for us. However, since it is free, there really is no reason to not list property there. Craigslist can be great for smaller and cheaper properties. The demographics of Craigslist are looking for bargains, so smaller, less expensive properties fit the Craigslist demographics. You will definitely get Craigslist leads, so it is important to take them seriously.

The above services ensure you will be listed in the proper areas to sell your properties. All of these services work together, so it is important to use them in conjunction with each other and not eliminate three because your first property sold off of the MLS. The great thing about these services is that people forward listings to other people. On Zillow, you will see the "saves" and "views" on your property, and anything that is shared is automatically "saved." Use these resources to help turn your properties as fast as possible.

How to Post

Now let's talk about how to post your property in more detail. The first thing you will want to do is select the photos you want to use. I usually select about six of them because that is what most sites allow you to post. Six has also been a great number for my company because it's not too few and not too many. Once your drone pilot sends you back the pictures, you will use those. Typically, you will want one with an outlined parcel as shown in the picture below which is usually the primary photo I use for a post, and it's the one people will see when scrolling Zillow—it will be the default image. You also will want to have some ground photos and more aerial photos as well. A good combination of both can make a big difference.

Another tactic you can do is use a tool called Boxbrownie.com. Box Brownie is a software that enhances photos for your listing. It will take a cloudy day and make it look sunny. It will take bad lighting and make it look good. It is a great tool to help grab people's eye. You do not need this on every picture, but for your default picture I recommend it. Remember, the more views, the more likely your parcel will sell.

Next you will need to write a good description. Since your land typically will not have an address because there has never been a structure on it, you will have to provide things like the parcel number, latitude and longitude, driving directions, and more. The goal of writing a legal description is to remove as many questions as you can and answer them in the property description. A great tool I use for property descriptions is ChatGPT. You can utilize ChatGPT in many areas of this business, and this is a great introduction to using it in your land business. Tell ChatGPT as much information as you can about the property and then give it direction to write the description. You can tell ChatGPT things like "keep it to five hundred words." Below is an example description of a property my company recently listed.

- *"Located in Bean Blossom Township, Monroe County, IN. This is a rare opportunity to own a piece of property on the White River with a beautiful view. This property would be the perfect weekend getaway. These two parcels back up to a hidden wooded hillside that towers over the White River. Access to the parcels is off of N Texas Ridge Road, down a private lane (W. Owl Lane). There is a small 480 sq foot single family dwelling built in 1950 that sits on the property. The current condition is not livable. The lots are located a short five-minute drive south of Gosport, Indiana and only twenty-five minutes from both Martinsville and Bloomington. Current condition of private well and septic is unknown. Buyer is responsible for own due-diligence. Property is being sold as-is. Monroe County, IN, Bean Blossom Township, N Texas Ridge Rd, Gosport, IN 47433. Each parcel is one acre for a total of two acres 53-03-06-400-018.000-001 and 53-03-06-400-012.000-001 Longitude/Latitude: (39.329992, -86.669918) GPS*

Coordinates: 39° 19' 47.9712" N86° 40' 11.7048" W 2022
Annual taxes $566.59 and $485.64"

As you see, it starts off like a sales pitch then leads into a lot of information. This is what you want. Now a potential buyer can read through that and find out if it's for them or not without calling or messaging you. Of course, you will still get calls, but the idea is to limit them with a lot of upfront transparent information. If you get a call for the same thing five to ten times, then it's probably a sign you need to add that information to your listing.

Once you have all the photos, property information, and description ready to go, you are now set to list the property. If you are using a Realtor, ignore this step as they do it for you, but I would highly encourage putting it on Facebook Marketplace and forwarding your Realtor the leads.

Realtor Versus Selling Yourself

As we discussed in this book, you have the ability to sell the properties yourself, or you can use a Realtor. For my company, we do about a fifty-fifty split between using a Realtor and listing ourselves. In this section we will go over the pros and cons of using a Realtor and talk about how to find the absolute best one in the area. That can be much easier said than done in rural America as good land Realtors are scarce.

When you have a purchase agreement on the acquisition side, at some point during title you typically make the decision if you are going to use a Realtor or not. A few things to consider while making this decision is your property size. If you have a $20,000 property, there is not a huge profit for your Realtor since they're paid on commission. Often, they will have a $2,500 minimum or $3,500 minimum per listing. That can eat into your margins since you have such a small property. However, it is still possible to list a small property with a Realtor, but most of them won't put the time and energy into it for such small returns. One way to overcome this is by selling them on your future value. Although this deal is small, you have many more big deals coming, and you'll want to work with one Realtor in the area for all of them. Personally, I like to sell smaller properties ourselves and bigger properties with Realtors.

Another thing to consider is whether you can find good land Realtors in the property's area. I like to look at other land listings and sold properties to find a Realtor. I typically call ten Realtors who have had listings in the area, and maybe three or four will call me back. The reason I call so many is because most don't call back. If they're not calling you back, they're not hungry for business. If they're not hungry for business, they're going to let buyers slip through the cracks. Bad Realtors are detrimental to the land investing business so spend a lot of time finding a good Realtor upfront. Once you list with them you are in a six month contract and it is hard to get out of. After you have received three to four call backs, you then have a decision to make.

Always ask the following questions when discussing listing a property in the area. First strike up a general conversation and let them know about the property you own and where it is.

Questions to Ask
- Do you cover the area my land is in?
- How far away from it are you?
- What is your commission structure?

- What is the contract length? (six months, eight months, one to two months.)
- How quickly can you list the property?
- Can you go to the property, and when can you go?
- What price do you think will help sell the property quickly? (This may take time for them to get back with you.)

Commission structure is the percentage they will take from the sold price. Depending on the size of the deal, you usually see 6 percent, 8 percent, and 10 percent. I think 8 percent is a good middle ground because they will split that with the other side if a Realtor comes in and they get 4 percent each. Anything above 10 percent is hefty, and probably not worth it. In a Realtor, you are not looking for the cheapest one, but you are looking for quality. The contract length is very important because if they lock you in a contract, you have to pay them a commission if it sells during that time. I always push for a six month contract, no longer. Our business is to turn properties quickly, and it should never take over six months.

The next question I ask them concerns their opinion about the best price for the property. Take this price opinion with a grain of salt because they are wrong more than they are right. But if you have a good Realtor that has a lot of land experience in the area, they are more likely to be good at this. I like to form my own price opinions, use the Realtor's opinion, use other land investors, and then come up with a conclusion. This price opinion gives the Realtor homework to do on the land and requires that they get back with you. If they never get back with you, don't use them.

Another question I ask is if they can visit the property, and when can they visit. You want to make sure your Realtors are visiting the property, especially the higher dollar ones. The last question I like to ask is how quickly they can list the property. Tell them you would like it listed by X date if possible. You do not want a Realtor taking three weeks to get it listed because, remember, speed is the name of the game.

Another strategy you can use is listing it yourself and if you have trouble selling it, then moving it to a Realtor. Sometimes Realtors can slow down the sales process due to being slow with posting, getting back to leads, etc. You can always get a Realtor involved if you list it yourself, but it is hard to get rid of one. They also can eat at the profit, which, if your margins are good, usually isn't a deal breaker. Overall, if you find a great Realtor, they can be a tremendous asset to your business. I continue to send mail to some Realtors' areas simply because they are so good and they make the selling process so easy. It takes a whole side of the business off your plate.

Answering Leads

Answering leads is more of a customer service job than a salesperson job. It is the process of answering emails, texts, calls and any inquiries regarding the sale of the property. Your job is to get back with them promptly with the correct answers. There are different levels of leads that you get, some very serious and some just fishing. Either way, it is important to answer all leads because you never know what can come of it. On Facebook Marketplace, having answers ready to go and copy and paste them in is best. Since it's such a large volume of leads, and most are not that serious, we want to be wise with our time. They will ask if it's still available, driving directions, if you take seller financing, and more. You will get the hang of it fairly quickly and will have answers ready to go. I personally like to review all leads at once and check a few times per day. Instead of replying to every Facebook lead instantly, I like to compile them and send responses at set times. Depending on how you work, you can adapt your own strategy. Land.com leads typically call or email. These are very serious leads, and you need to make sure to get back with them quickly. The main takeaway from this section is to answer leads promptly. No need to put your sales hat on for this role, treat it more of a customer service role where your job is to answer questions and follow up as needed. There will be times you don't know the answers, and that is okay. You can give them a call back later. The worst thing you can do is act like you know the answer and then be wrong. Be upfront, tell them you're unsure, but you'll get back with them later.

The last thing to discuss in this section is creating a buyers list. If you have buyers you talk to on the phone who are interested in land, but not yours specifically, create a buyers list. Over time, this can grow, and you can sell properties using it. Perhaps somebody is interested in land but wants a pond, or more road frontage. Your land will not be for every land buyer, so when having these conversations make sure to get contact information so you can send them information about the properties.

Seller Financing

As we've already covered, seller financing is when the seller of the property provides a financing option to the buyer. The terms of the financing, typically negotiated between the buyer and the seller of the property, include the down payment, interest rate, repayment schedule, loan length and more. The typical loan length that I have seen is around six years, at a 10 percent interest. Interest rates change as the market changes, but keep in mind these sellers are getting seller financing typically because they do not qualify to get financing through their bank. So, in general, you are dealing with less-qualified buyers who are a higher risk and, as a result, have higher interest rates.

The plus side of seller financing is it opens up a larger pool of potential buyers and makes the land more accessible to those who don't have access to great credit or funds. It can also help you sell it more quickly. The downside is you now have to service the loan, or you can sell the loan. If you service the loan, you will need to get a software or service that helps with this. Servicing notes can be great steady cash flow from the monthly payments which include the principal plus interest. If the seller defaults, you will be protected and typically be able to take the land back. This all depends on the way you structure the land financing. One way to structure it is through a deed of trust, which is a legal document commonly used in real estate that involves seller financing. In a deed of trust there are three parties involved:

1. Trustor (buyer): The entity purchasing the property through seller financing. They sign the deed of trust, which serves as a pledge of the property as security, or the financing provided by the seller.

2. Beneficiary (seller): The entity providing funding.

3. Trustee: a neutral third party responsible for holding the legal title to the property on behalf of the seller. The trustee acts as a custodian of the property and is typically a title company.

A deed of trust is used to secure the sellers' interest in the property until the buyer fulfills their obligation under the financial agreement. The deed of trust outlines various provisions, including the property's legal description, the amount financed, the interest rate, repayment terms, and any other conditions agreed upon between the buyer and the seller. It also specifies the circumstances under which the trustee can initiate foreclosure proceedings if the buyer defaults on their payments. Upon successful completion of the financing agreement, the trustee releases the deed of trust, and the buyer obtains full ownership of the property.

There are different types of land seller financing out there, and it is important to explore your options. As a matter of fact, there are complete books on seller financing.

One other type of seller financing used is called a land contract. A land contract is similar to a deed of trust with how it is structured, but the legality behind it changes. In a land contract, the seller retains legal ownership of the property until the buyer fulfills their obligation under the contract. The buyer takes positions and equitable interest in the property but does not receive immediate title. The main difference is the process if it defaults. For land contracts, the contract can simply be terminated by the seller with no legal proceeding. For a deed of trust, it goes through a foreclosure process which is different in each state. In general, land contracts are usually more favorable for sellers, but some states are cracking down on them so make sure to talk with title companies and attorneys on how to structure this for your area.

If you decide to explore the seller financing route, you can sell your "notes," which is essentially the mortgage or seller financing package. There are buyers of land notes out there who like to get cash flow from servicing and collecting the payments every month. Note investors usually pay 70 – 80 percent of unpaid principal balance. Below is some basic math to walk you through it.

- Purchase price: $100,000
- Down Payment: $20,000
- Loan Balance after Down Payment: $80,000
- Interest rate: 10 percent

To keep things simple, if they paid you 80 percent of unpaid principal balance you would get $64,000. You also would have the down payment so you would have a total of $64,000 + $20,000 = $84,000. Yes, you lost 16 percent of your deal, but at least you sold it and if you're following along our strategy, you should have margins to play with.

- Purchase price: $100,000
- Down Payment: $20,000
- Loan Balance after Down Payment: $80,000
- Investor pays you: $64,000
- Total sale price after investor payout: $84,000 (including down payment you collected)

Now let's talk about if we were to service it ourselves—you would make more than your sale price, but you wouldn't get this money upfront; it would be over the course of several years. If you were to amortize this for five years at 10 percent, the $80,000 would turn to $101,986. When adding back the down payment that is $121,986 and you would receive that in monthly, quarterly, or annual payments depending on how you structured it.

Wrap Up

To summarize this chapter, it is important to get the highest quality posting in as many places as possible. Facebook Marketplace, MLS, Land.com are essential to your success. If you are using a Realtor, make sure to spend time finding the right one. Call around and ask the questions we discussed in this chapter. There are advantages to using a Realtor, but they also commit you to a contract, and if they don't perform well, a contract is difficult to get out of. Answering leads when selling your property is more like a customer success job than a sales job, but nonetheless, responding promptly and answering all their questions is crucial. While exploring seller financing options, it is important to discuss options with local experts as this is a legal matter.

12
REVIEWING CONTRACTS

Got an Offer, Now What?

Since you're listed in the appropriate places with the appropriate price and marketing, you should soon be receiving some buyer interest and offers. Whether you get an offer the first day or the eighth week, it all depends how the market reacts to the property. It is very hard to predict the success of every single piece of land since there are so many variables like location, size, lay of the land, price, attributes and more. Everything we do up to this point is an educated prediction, which can be fairly accurate, but you never truly know until the property is listed for sale.

When you receive an offer, take your time reviewing it. Not all offers are good offers, and just because the offer price is high, that does not mean it's a homerun offer. There are many things to look at like duration of closing, due diligence, if they want a survey, if they want a perc test, the earnest money deposit amount, and more. By combining all of the factors, including price, we can counter, decline, or accept the offer. Land offers will occasionally fall out, especially if you are not vetting the buyers enough. There are people who make offers who simply can't afford it or are just fishing for a good deal. We want to make sure to get contracts with legitimate, serious buyers only. This will be a shock to some of you, but analyzing offers as a skeptic is sometimes the best way to go. Deals that fall through typically do so because of contingencies. Contingencies are anything that need to be done for this property to close. There will be times we take a much lower offer with fewer contingencies because we know that it will close and it's a very serious buyer. In this chapter we will discuss what to look for in an offer and which ones to accept to best guarantee you the most profit.

Take your time when reviewing offers because there typically is no reason to automatically accept the first offer. Always analyze the other interested property buyers. If you just listed a property and it is getting an offer the week of posting, always look for more offers coming in. If your property has been sitting for ninety days with very little interest, that is different. When you get very little interest you have to take all offers very seriously, even if they have a lot of contingencies.

Reviewing Contracts

Reviewing contracts is a rather boring task, for me at least, but a very important step in the sales process. There are key details in each contract that you will need to look at in more depth. If you are using a Realtor, use them for advice and to help you. Contracts can be overwhelming at first, but once you know 90 percent of it is fluff, then you'll quickly learn how to locate the 10 percent that matters, and it gets easier. Things you want to look for are perc tests, due diligence timeline, surveys, financing, and any other contingencies. We will discuss those in detail in the next section.

Another major factor you'll want to consider while analyzing an offer is the amount of time to close. I have seen anywhere from a one-week close to a four-month close. Sometimes people will try to get a long closing period so they can sell their other assets and/ or do due diligence on the property. We want offers that are likely to close, and four months typically is too long for us to consider. The average closing timeframe is about one month, but you will have cash offers come in with a two-week timeframe every once in a while. Usually those buyers have already done their due diligence and don't need any perc test, or anything else done with the land before closing. Those are the offers we love.

The first thing to look at while reviewing the agreement to buy and sell real estate will be to identify the purchase price. I personally like to open up a separate document to summarize the offer to get rid of all the fluff. In my separate document I will identify the purchase price and write that down. The next thing you want to look at is the financing, typically it will say finance or cash. If it is finance, you want to make sure they have a pre-approval and/or funds ready to go. The next thing you want to identify is the earnest money. Earnest money is a sum of money provided by the buyer to demonstrate a sincere intention to purchase the property or enter the agreement. When a buyer submits an offer, they typically include an earnest money deposit as part of the process. Without this they do not have skin in the game. The earnest money is typically held by the title company or Realtor and goes toward the purchase of the land at closing. It is held by a third party because if they buyer backs out for no given reason, the seller can keep the earnest money (if structured appropriately and depending on contingencies.) If they back out for a reason that was stated in the contract, then they will recoup their earnest money. An example is if they had a perc test contingency, and the perc test failed, they would get their money back. The higher the earnest money the better, but it is typically 1 – 5 percent of the purchase price.

The next thing you want to look at is the closing costs; sometimes they will try to put all the closing costs on your side, which may or may not be what was agreed upon. This is usually under a section called transaction costs but can look different on different contract templates. Next you'll want to look at the finance section. Typically it will state that the buyer's obligation under this contract is or is not contingent on getting a loan. There will be more information stated in this section like how soon they have to apply for financing and the final date when the loan must be closed. Put all of this information in your separate document.

Next, let's take a look at the survey provision in the contract. Always look to see if there is a land survey contingency which can delay the deal closing by six to eight weeks, depending on the area. If the surveyors in the area are backed up, this can really delay the closing. You want to make sure to get this timeframe if they do have a survey contingency. I personally don't like survey clauses or perc test clauses because they can delay the transactions.

One of the most important areas to look at is the due diligence section. You want to see what the due diligence provision says, but the contract typically will say due diligence begins on x date at x time and ends on X date at X time. You want a short due diligence period, because this is a time where they can essentially backout for no reason. Due diligence is such a broad term it essentially allows the other party to backout of the contract for no given reason. Usually seven to fourteen days is standard; if they ask for longer, there is always an opportunity to counter.

Next you want to look at the soil and water test section. The soil test for land is referring to the perc test we have discussed. Perc tests are more serious for smaller properties. If you have a five-acre (or larger) property, they typically are not needed. If they have a perc test contingent on the contract, this is another area you can counter.

To sum up reviewing an offer, you have to understand that the more contingencies, the more likelihood the buyer will fall out. After you compile your offer breakdown document, you can review it and get a feel for all of the information you have, and counter based on that. Below is an example of how my team does it.

Offer Breakdown:

- $79,000.00 Cash
- No Closing expense to seller
- Closing date 7/28/2023 (Four weeks away)
- $1000.00 earnest money to be held by the title company and to be paid within three days of a binding agreement
- Thirty day due diligence
- Buyer has right to get perc test
- At closing, seller shall pay 4 percent commission of purchase price to selling broker.

- Buyer shall have the option of doing a new survey of property at Buyer's expense during the due diligence period.

Our listing price for this property was $90,000 and it had only been listed a day when we got this offer. We were getting five to six phone calls on it a day and it was a very hot property. Since it was this hot, I knew we had more leverage, and I was willing to risk this offer to hold out for better ones. We knew we would get asking price offers coming in with lower contingencies. Below is how we countered.

Counter Breakdown

- $85,000 Cash
- No closing expense to seller
- Closing data 7/28/2023 (no changes made)
- $2,500 earnest money
- Ten day due diligence
- No perc tests

This is generally how your counteroffer will go. Many times they will say no, or you will meet somewhere in the middle between their offer and your counter. The main takeaway from our offer is we are getting more earnest money, less due diligence time, and no perc test. If this offer had been sitting on the market eight weeks with no offers, I would have countered much more lightly, but the fact is we were getting blown up on this posting and we knew we had leverage. The more leverage you have the more you can counter and negotiate without much risk. The risk here was them saying no and us finding another buyer quickly, which was very minimal.

Managing Realtors and Title

Once you accept an offer, you will have to manage the title process similar to how we did on the acquisition side. I am usually not as aggressive on this side, but I make sure to pay attention to the important dates that were mentioned on the contract, such as financing application date, perc test completion, survey dates, and more. The reason I do this is so we can follow up on those dates to make sure they're being completed on time. When there is another Realtor representing the buyer, you will contact the Realtor instead of the actual buyer. Everything on this will filter through the Realtor. If there is no Realtor, then contact the buyer per usual. Same goes for you if you are using a Realtor to sell your property; they would be responsible to contact the other side. It would be your job to contact your Realtor and ask for updates. No need to be overbearing on this side; you just want to make sure it's on track to close.

There will be times buyers fall out and dates change. Typically if a closing date needs to change, they will have you sign an addendum, which pretty much is a legal document saying they are changing the date. When they request to change a date, it is always important to find out why. There will be times they keep extending the deadline for no apparent reason and the deal is likely to fall out. You want to prevent these situations and make sure they just need a little extra time to get a loan or whatever the situation is. If a buyer does fall out and you lose them, it is not the end of the world. If this was a hot property that got a lot of interest before, it should get more interest again when you relist it. Make sure that even when it is under contract, you are taking down names and contact numbers just in case the current contract falls through. Go back to your buyers list if you have one and start calling them to inform them. Occasionally they will be skeptical of why it fell through but let them know whatever the reason was. Typically it is that the buyers didn't have the money or couldn't get a loan. This is a great way to utilize your buyers list and take advantage of all the calls you got early on or after your property was under contract to sell.

Closings

I personally have never been to a closing in person, so I am going to assume you won't either. Since this business is remote let's take advantage of that and close remotely. When the title company is approaching closing dates, you will need to get a date on the schedule and get your mobile notary lined up. Call your seller or Realtor and organize a time to close with them and/or the title company. If there are no Realtors involved, you will work directly with the title company and buyer on when they are available or good to close. If they are closing remotely, you can organize another mobile notary for them as well, but title companies will sometimes do this for you. You want to check with the title company on this to see what their process is.

Another key thing to look out for here is the closing documents. You will want to review the closing document just like we did on the buy side, except this time there is more room for error. Since there are often time contingencies, Realtors, surveys, etc., you will want to make sure your final settlement statement and/or HUD look good. Read through each line item on your HUD to make sure it makes sense. We catch errors in about 50 percent of our closing documents, and you want to catch them early so they can adjust them and not delay closing. If the contract said buyer and seller are to split closing costs, make sure they were properly split. If it shows the buyer pays, make sure they are paying for it. You will catch mistakes on your closing documents eventually, so it is important to take it seriously. It could be an easy $800 mistake otherwise.

Finally, after you have notarized the documents and sent them back in, you get paid. You will get paid directly from the title company and they typically wire it to your bank. They can also issue checks, but I always like wires because it's easier, quicker, and more secure. You can find out how much you are being paid by looking at the settlement statement or HUD and look at the bottom of the document. It typically says something like "cash to seller," and that is the final amount after the taxes, Realtors' fees, closing costs and anything else you paid for during closing.

Wrap Up

It is important to take every offer seriously and review the details of the offer. People will fish for really good deals and try to put in too many contingencies. Remember, the more contingencies, the more likely it will fall out. Keep Chapter 12 nearby when you get offers back to review because it takes time to understand all these issues. Finally, when selling the property, make sure to follow up with the other party to ensure the dates are being met and closing will be on time. Review every HUD statement as a skeptic and try to find things wrong with it: it can save you a lot of money.

13

WHAT TO DO WITH YOUR PROFITS

Congrats! You Made a Profit!

Now that you have finally bought and sold a property, you have officially made a profit. The first time is always the hardest, but after you get more deals done, it becomes like clockwork. It is important to continue to educate yourself even though you may feel like you have it figured out after one deal. Now, since you have earned a profit, it's important to disburse an appropriate amount early on to ensure you're investing in the growth of the business and future. Time after time, I see people putting their money in the wrong places. Although it might sound great to keep that profit for yourself, it is essential to reinvest it to grow the business exponentially. Especially at first. Trust me—if you reinvest it correctly, there is much more profit that will be available in the future. In this chapter, we are going to discuss how to best utilize your money and reinvest it in the right areas.

Try New Things

Try new things. Don't be scared to think for yourself. You don't have to follow everything that is in this book or that your mentors do. If you're not texting and you want to text, this is the time to go for it. If you're texting or cold calling and want to send mail, you now have the profits to do so. I like to take around 10 percent of my budget and invest it in new areas exploring different ways to do it. Try sending out some neutral letters with no price on them. Try remailing counties and areas you already targeted ninety days ago. Or try ranged offers. These are offers that have a price range instead of a set price. For example: "We will buy your property anywhere between $15,000 – $28,000."

Trying these new methods will allow you to acquire deals that you wouldn't have gotten necessarily from a blind offer like we originally sent. We want to find more effective ways to reach landowners, and most methods can be good methods if executed right. If you don't get results from the first time doing something, make sure to give it a good chance. For all of these methods you need a big enough sample size to make good decisions. Each one will have its pros and cons, but overall you will be able to acquire more properties than you did by only using one method.

Subdivisions

Subdividing has been a big part of my land investing success, especially this year, in 2024. I love subdivides for two reasons; they are larger deals which means more profit, and they provide tremendous value to sellers of the land and the future buyers. Let me explain.

Minor subdivisions are the act of buying a large property— let's say sixty acres for this example—and then dividing that sixty-acre block into multiple parcels. They are minor because they do not require engineering or infrastructure. Depending on how the land lays, we might chop it up into twelve separate five-acre lots. This is the same philosophy as bulk purchasing—if you buy one hundred hotdogs at Costco, you're going to get a much better price per unit than if you buy one hotdog at a baseball game. This applies to land, too—the more land you buy the better price per acre you will get. The five-acre parcels in the example above may be worth $45,000 each. But the sixty acres as a single purchase might be worth $300,000. By splitting the parcel up into smaller lots, you create more value—your sixty acres are now worth $540,000 instead of $300,000, just by dividing them up into twelve lots.

This also works in favor of the seller because instead of sending an offer letter to buy the sixty acres for 40 percent of market value—like we traditionally do—we can now make an offer based on *the future value* of around $540,000. I would feel comfortable paying 70 percent or more of market value for a property like this. If we offer $220,000 that is about 75 percent of the market value of $300,000. Naturally, you will get more sellers interested when you can pay that much and still close very quickly with cash. There is now $320,000 of profit in this deal and I'm paying 75 percent of market value, which is much more than the usual flip. So you are providing a ton of value to both the sellers, the future buyers, and yourself by splitting it up into multiple parcels. Everybody wins!

Before offering on a subdivide, you will want to check out the minor subdivision laws with the county. Often you can just type into Google "X County Minor Subdivision Laws" and their zoning restrictions will come up. You should also always verify with the county before executing your plan. There are three questions you should always ask:

1. How many parcels can I split a lot into to keep it a minor subdivide?

2. What is the minimum acreage I can split a lot into?

3. Are there any restrictions created when splitting a lot?

In some cases, a county will not allow you to split any lot into more than five parcels, which would ruin my plan for the example above and would make me rethink what I could offer for it. That means the most I could do is split it into five twelve-acre lots. Another common response is that you cannot split any lot into parcels smaller than five acres. Finally, the county will detail any restrictions for the land if you split the lot up, like what type of structures would and would not be allowed on different lot sizes.

The logistics of minor subdivides is usually pretty simple. I typically just split the parcel up along the road so I don't need to create roads myself—that can get tricky and costly. You will also need a survey on the land to show the surveyor your plan. Call a bunch of surveyors in the area and get a quote and a timeframe they can do it in. Some will be three months out and some can do it next week. You can also call the county or city to ask who they recommend. For larger surveys, expect to pay $10,000 or more. It sounds like a lot, but we're adding hundreds of thousands of dollars of value. Once the survey is complete, they will file the survey with the county and each lot will now have its own unique parcel number.

Last year we purchased seventy acres in Tate County, Mississippi. We purchased the land for $135,000. The market value at the time was around $190,000, so we paid about 70 percent of that. We closed this deal in cash in only a few weeks because we had a plan to subdivide it. Right after we got the property under contract, we contacted a Realtor in the area who we had used previously to get some insights into the market and price.

Originally, we were planning on splitting these lots into a mixture of five- and ten-acre lots. But after we asked the county the above questions, we found out we could not split the lots into under ten acres without restrictions being added. The county said any parcel under ten acres would not be allowed to have a single-wide mobile home. This rule would have significantly affected my pool of potential buyers. Since the lot was in Mississippi, we knew mobile homes in rural areas were a large part of the real estate market, and so we decided to keep every parcel over ten acres. Our Realtor and the research we did ourselves indicated we could sell each ten-acre lot for between $40,000 and $50,000. The survey cost us about $10,000.

Below is the survey of the seventy acres subdivide in Tate County.

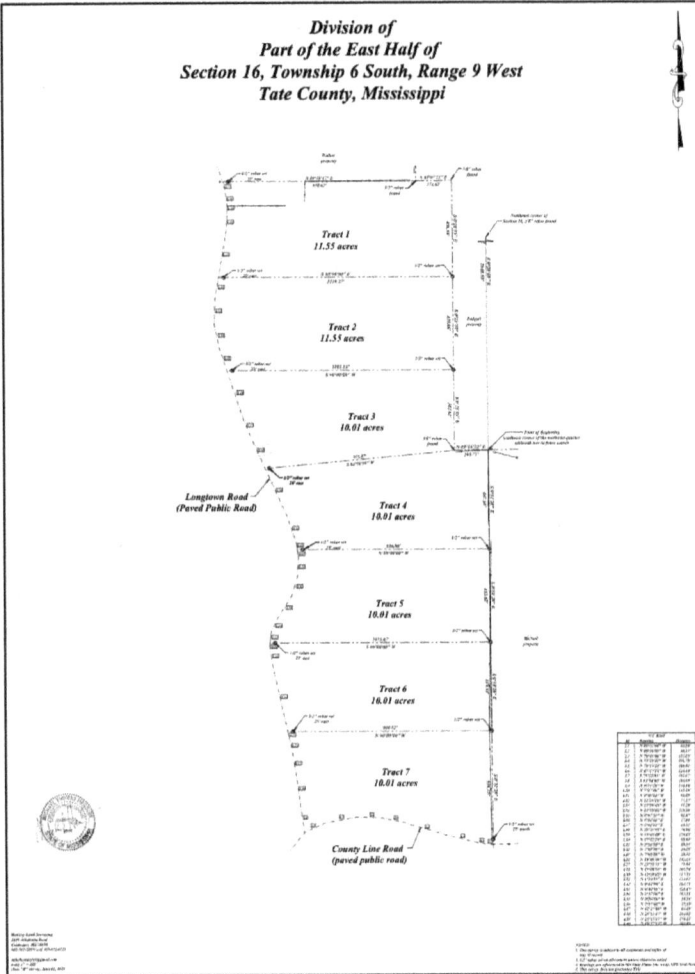

Division of
Part of the East Half of
Section 16, Township 6 South, Range 9 West
Tate County, Mississippi

Tract 1
11.55 acres

Tract 2
11.55 acres

Tract 3
10.01 acres

Longtown Road
(Paved Public Road)

Tract 4
10.01 acres

Tract 5
10.01 acres

Tract 6
10.01 acres

Tract 7
10.01 acres

County Line Road
(paved public road)

After closing on the land, we listed the individual parcels and sold a few immediately. We got most of our initial investment of $135,000 back very quickly. This is the nice thing about subdivides—you can "break even" just by selling a couple of the lots. After a few months, we had sold all the lots for around $450,000 total. We were able to increase the value by over 100 percent, and knowing this is what allowed us to offer the seller more money in our initial offer. This is why I love subdividing; it is very sustainable!

Investing in Your Own Deals

The next thing you may want to consider after selling your first property is investing in your own deals. Investing in your own deal can be a great way to increase your profit per deal. Most people can't do this at first, but after you sell your first deal, depending on the size, it could be possible. There are pros and cons of investing in your own deals. The number one thing to consider is making sure it doesn't eat into your marketing dollars. If you invest in your own deal but lose your money to send mail for future deals, then that will be a bad investment. If you have enough money to do both, then great. If you have a homerun deal, which will come, investing in your own deal can be a great way to get to the next level.

Another con of investing in your own deal is that you now possess all of the risk. When you get traditional deal funding, the funder takes on the risk. If you buy your deal, it's your money therefore it's your risk. That is why it's very important to do such thorough and in-depth due diligence on every property you buy. Overall, investing in your deals is a great thing, but make sure to still get mentors and other land investors' opinions.

Investing in Other Deals

The next thing you can look to do is invest in other people's deals. In this instance you would be considered the "investor" or the "deal funder." When you have enough excess money to not only buy your own deals while still having plenty of mail money, then this can also be a great time to leverage your land knowledge and invest in others' deals. Make sure to let people know you are interested in funding so when they have deals that need an investor, you come to mind. It is fairly easy getting into the deal funding side of the business.

There are pros and cons of deal funding, and below you'll find a few that come to mind:

Pros:

- Scalable: Deal funding is very scalable. You can get five to ten more deals without doing work. That is because the manager or the person who needs the funding finds and sells the deal. Your job is to wire money.
- Profitable: If you do it right, deal funding can be very profitable. You can be selective with the kind of deals you accept based on what you are comfortable with. Just because you are funding deals does not mean you need to have a million dollars. You can start by doing deals under $50,000 if you're more comfortable with that.

Cons:

- Risk: Since you are putting up the money, you take on the risk. Being an expert in land is crucial and you want to be able to underwrite the deals.
- Control: Since you are not in charge of the deal, you lose control. Your success is based off the manager. So pick the people you want to work with carefully. They are just as important as the deal itself.

Keep in mind that while considering deal funding, it is important to look at each deal as if it's your own. Just because somebody told you it's a good deal does not mean it is. Take it through the standard due diligence process and underwrite the property. Make sure they provide you with their due diligence as well. There are two sides of deal funding that you need to underwrite, the manager and the deal. You can have a bad manager and a great deal, and it makes it very difficult. On the other side, you can have a bad deal and great manager. You want to make sure to choose the people whom you are working with very wisely. Bad managers can take too long to sell the property, be unresponsive, and ultimately kill the profitability of the deal. Work with people who work hard and want the same success as you. I love hungry managers; they are the best to work with. They get the property posted quickly, provide updates, and sell the properties faster.

Invest in Software

Another thing to look into while you are scaling up your land business is software. The land investing business model can get chaotic as you start pushing seven- and eight-figure business models. You want to make sure you have the proper software and CRMs. At Land Investing Online, we created a CRM for land investors to help keep their land business organized. This is currently what we use, and it tracks the whole business from the lead to selling the property. It is also great with tracking financials of the business to keep track of your profit and money. There is plenty of other software out there that can help you scale your business.

I have even hired consultants to help scale the software side of the business. They have helped customize our workflows and implement new systems. There are almost always more efficient ways to do things. At first this may seem hard and farfetched but, trust me, putting your money into better and easier ways of doing things can really pay off in the long run. Is it going to pay off today? No, but over the course of five years, the return on good software and consultants can help tremendously.

Invest in Education

Continuous learning is part of a core value at my companies. I strongly believe in the ability to move forward slightly every single day. Continuous learning allows you to make it feel easy after doing it for a while. One way to do this is by investing in education, coaches, books, YouTube, etc. I like to focus on *one thing* until I get there. If you take your focus off land investing before you reach your goal, then this will heavily influence your long-term success. Once you hit seven-figures, or wherever you want to go, then start exploring new real estate models, long term rentals, other business ideas, or whatever it is you want. Alex Hormozi, one of my favorite marketers said, "A focused fool can accomplish more than a distracted genius." I love this quote and couldn't agree more. In the Land Investing Online community I see too many people looking in too many directions. Until that one thing is done, everything else is a distraction. Gary Keller wrote a book called *The One Thing* and it was eye opening for me. He talked about how all the very influential entrepreneurs focused on *one thing*. Elon Musk, Jeff Bezos, Steve Jobs, Mark Zuckerburg all focused on one thing until they got to their goal. This especially hit home for me because I had over ten businesses in a very short span. Although I was able to achieve a good deal of success off a few of them, what would the results have been if I only focused on my one electric bike company? The tradeoffs are often not worth it.

Another thing continuous education allows you to do is stay on top of trends and see what is working. As time changes, businesses change with it. What if mail yields stopped working and you had to adapt to a new method of acquiring. Education teaches you how to do this, but it also provides you with insights about the changes, so, hopefully, you can get ahead of these changes and implement them before it's too late.

Scaling Your Business

Scaling your business is one of the most fun, but also challenging things you can do. I always say it's easy to make a $1 million dollar land business, but can you make a $10 million dollar business? The reason for that is simple, you need systems, processes, and most importantly, great people around you. Great people are the hardest challenge. If you have hired people before, you know how challenging this can be. Not only do they need to be capable, but they need to fit the culture and mission as well. Reinvesting into people that need real salaries can be tricky and scary at first. This is why having mentors can be so critical. The first person I ever hired was a transaction coordinator who did a little bit of everything. The name transaction coordinator refers to managing the buying and selling side of the business, but as a small business you need versatile people. This transaction coordinator also was in charge of postings, answering sales leads, updating certain aspects of the website, along with title and closings, reviewing docs, and more. I think this is a great first position to hire.

Another position you want to consider is a virtual assistant.

They can help you scrub your data, pull comps, organize, and reply to emails and much more. The great thing about virtual assistants is they are affordable. I see virtual assistants being paid from $3/hour to $6/hour on the high end. The cost of living in their countries is much lower than ours, and they can live comfortably off of that. I have always hired my virtual assistants from the Philippines, but you can look into other areas as well. I have been very happy with hiring virtual assistants, but I treat them like any employee and make sure they fit the culture. My mentor always tells me "hire slow, fire fast." One person can ruin the culture of the business if they have toxic tendencies.

Another position to consider when moving forward is a salesperson. Salespeople are one of the hardest positions to find and manage in my experience. Yes, there are a lot of salespeople out there, but finding the right one for this business has been hard. In the past, I have had my salespeople be in charge of the acquisition process and the disposition process, essentially buying and selling the land. I paid them a percentage-based commission, so they are incentivized to buy cheap and sell high. If you have a partner or somebody who fits the job who can do it part time, that can be best at first. But it is also really difficult to find.

The last position to hire while scaling up is a data analyst to price your mail and formulate your offers. To keep a data analyst busy, you need to have a heavy volume of offers being sent out. I know some people who use data analysts to also do other aspects of the business, such as formulating offers when leads come back without one.

Now that you have the foundation of the business, you can rinse and repeat. Always continue to focus on hiring the right people, because they can make or break your business while scaling up. Once you no longer have to scrub data and price mail and answer every lead, you can put your time into things that can really grow your business, like hiring, firing, managing your employees, and creating better systems. That is the ultimate growth strategy— outsource whatever is sucking up your time so you can focus on growing the business.

Wrap Up

After you sell your property, you will have profit which opens up the door to reinvestments. Investing in the right direction is crucial to scaling up your business. The first place to always reinvest is mail and marketing, because that is how we make profit. The next place to reinvest is buying your own deals, and eventually getting into deal funding for other people's deals. Try new things, look into subdividing properties, and explore other niches. Eventually it will be time to invest in systems, process, and employees, which can help take your business to the next level. This allows you to outsource tasks you no longer need to do and to open up your time to be focused on more important things.

14
ACCOUNTING

Keeping your accounting organized from the beginning is important so you don't have to play catch up for your taxes later. It is also important to understand your numbers and financial performance to keep track of how you're doing. Over time, you will see your profit continue to climb. It is important to work with an accountant and verify everything in this chapter. I am not an accountant, but I will share with you some of what I've learned over the past several years in land investing.

Inventory Versus Capital Gains

A very common question I get is about the capital gains tax of land investing. The short answer is we are not taxed on capital gains, but we are taxed as ordinary income since we engage in the business of buying and selling land for profit. In this case, the Internal Revenue Service (IRS) considers land flipping activities as an ordinary trade or business rather than an investment activity.

As a result, the profits you generate from selling the land would likely be subject to ordinary income tax rates rather than capital gains tax rates.

The distinction between ordinary income and capital gains is important for tax purposes. Generally, capital gains are derived from the sale of assets held for investment or personal use, such as stocks, bonds, or real estate held for a certain period of time. On the other hand, ordinary income is typically derived from regular business activities, employment, or services provided.

The IRS considers various factors to determine whether an activity qualifies as a trade or business, or an investment. These factors include the frequency and continuity of your land flipping transactions, the time and effort you devote to the activity, your intent at the time of acquisition (whether it was for investment or resale), and your expertise and knowledge in the real estate market.

If the IRS determines that your land flipping activities constitute a trade or business, the profit you make from selling the land would generally be taxed as ordinary income. The land itself would be treated as inventory or a cost of goods sold (COGS) because it is considered a part of your business inventory. This means that the cost of acquiring the land would be deducted as an expense when calculating your taxable income.

The good thing about this is since it is taxed as COGS, we have tons of write-offs to keep track of. Some of these include payrolls, mail, and software. Once you hire employees, payroll will almost always be your number one expense. Until then, it is important to keep your business lean. From my experience, once you start making good money it can be easy to let it get out of control.

However, it's important to note that tax laws can be complex and subject to change. The specific circumstances of your land investing business, such as the duration of ownership, the frequency of transactions, and any other relevant factors, can impact how your activities are classified for tax purposes. It's always advisable to consult with a tax professional or accountant who can provide personalized advice based on your specific situation and the current tax laws in effect.

Bookkeeping

Bookkeeping is a straightforward process for many people. You'll want to set up your books once you start actively buying and selling properties. I personally have always used QuickBooks, but there are plenty of others out there. I would not worry about setting up your books too early, and here are a few reasons why it is important to set up legitimate bookkeeping:

- Financial management: Effective bookkeeping allows you to track and manage your financial transactions, income, and expenses related to your land investing activities. It provides you with a clear overview of your financial health, helps you make decisions and plan for the future. By organizing and analyzing your financial data, you can make decisions on how much mail to send, when you can use money to buy your own deals, and if you're deal funding it will help you make decisions on how much capital to use, etc.

- Compliance with tax regulations: Maintaining accurate and up to date books is essential for meeting your tax obligations. It helps ensure that you report your income and expenses correctly.

Although there are several other reasons to set up your books, financial management and compliance with taxes are the main two. It can be tricky and take time setting up your books. I recommend outsourcing it to a professional as they are affordable and know what they are doing. If you want to do them yourself there are tons of free QuickBooks classes that you can take to learn.

After your books are set up, you can choose to do it monthly. That includes your monthly P&L statement (profit and loss) and your balance sheet. They can also customize any information for you that you need. Make sure to always double check your bookkeeper's work as they will miss things and not understand the business like you do. There is a learning curve for them, and it will take some time going back and forth.

S-Corp Versus LLC

At first, I almost always create an LLC for my businesses. If you are actively flipping land, you will want to make sure you are not doing it in your name anymore. As I mentioned earlier in the book, you can start by doing it in your name but once you get some deals under your belt, you will want to file for an LLC. Once you have your LLC and make a substantial amount of money, talk to your accountant about filing as an S-corporation. There are many pros and cons for filing an S-Corp, but the main advantage is there are tax benefits. One thing to note is that both LLCs and

S-Corporations are pass-through entities. This means the profit and losses pass through to your individual tax return. So if you made $100,000 in your nine-to-five job, and $100,000 net profit in your business, you would be personally taxed on $200,000 in both cases. But there are some benefits to a S-Corp that you will not see in a standard LLC. Here are some of the pros and cons of filing as an S-Corp.

Pros:

- Tax benefits: S-Corps can offer potential tax advantages. S-Corp shareholders (yourself) who are actively involved in the business may be able to save on self-employment taxes. You can split your salary between salary (subject to payroll tax) and distributions (not subject to payroll tax). In an LLC your whole income would be subject to payroll tax. A lot of money can be saved by escaping payroll tax through an S-Corp. In order to do this you will need to set up payroll.

Cons:

- Stricter compliance. S-Corps have more formalities and ongoing compliance obligations than LLCs. Talk to your accountant on the formalities and compliance you will need to abide by. It is nothing too stressful, but something to note.
- Accounting fees: I have been charged more for filing for a S-Corp than for an LLC. There is a cost to filing for this and since there are more regulations, you want to

make sure to do it through an accountant. LLCs are easy to file yourself, but I would not recommend doing that with an S-Corp.

Analyze your situation in November and make a decision about going to an S-Corp or staying as an LLC. It typically comes down to the profit you make in the business. A good guideline is if you make $100,000 or more then you'll want to file as an S-Corp. By November, you should be able to roughly calculate that and see how much you have made and will make by December 31. If you decide to go the S-Corp route, you will need to start payroll and give yourself a minimal salary. Talk to your accountant as to what can qualify for your minimal salary.

Know Your Numbers

Reviewing your numbers on a monthly basis can make a big difference in your land investing career. This is so crucial because it allows you to make informed decisions, mitigate risks, and maximize your profits. Here are a few reasons why knowing your financial situation is important:

- Investment evaluation: Understanding your financial numbers helps you evaluate the investment opportunity effectively. You can analyze what deals are best suited for using deal funding versus funding yourself.
- Profitability assessment: Knowing your financial numbers enables you to estimate potential profits accurately. It also helps you understand what is working and where to put your focus.

- Financial planning: Knowing your financial numbers enables you to calculate how much mail you can send, when you can hire a full time position, and how much you can reinvest overall into the business.

Knowing your financial numbers is vital for land investing because it enables you to evaluate the investment opportunity, assess profitability, create a realistic budget, manage risks, and enhance your ability to secure future partnerships.

Wrap Up

Once you start making a decent profit, it is vital to get a respected accountant on your team. Once you have a good accountant, you can make a decision together if you want to become an S-corporation or remain an LLC. Bookkeeping is vital for this business to understand the health and profitability of your company, manage risk, and understand how much you can reinvest. Knowing your numbers can help you manage the business and make high-level decisions.

APPENDICES

Drone Pictures Shot List (This is what we order from our Drone Pilots)**

2 street level pictures (taken on opposite side of street facing property)
2 street level pictures looking down the street
2 50 ft pictures taken from opposite side of street facing land (have street in picture from)
2 100 ft pictures taken from opposite side of street facing land (have street in picture from)
8 photos 350-400ft cardinal points
8 photos 150 feet to 200 cardinal points
3 photos tree line level straight on
1 photo birds eye
1-2 aerial photos with property outlined **IMPORTANT

Pictures with a normal camera throughout the land with different aspects of the property, trees, fence, surrounding area, anything else that could help with a real estate posting as we do not visit the properties ourselves. Any property notes as well are helpful.
**We need pilot to confirm the property's slope (i.e, need to check that there is enough level land for placing mobile/building).
***Address in the listing is not exact. Please refer to the GPS

(your company)
(your address)
(your city), (your state) (your zip)

Reference # (Reference)

Dear (First Name),

Have you considered selling your Land in **(County) County, (Situs St)?**

My company makes cash offers on vacant land all around the country. We specialize in quick and easy cash transactions. You do not have to deal with realtors, closing costs, or a long waiting period.

We can close in as little as **10-15 business days!!**

On the following page, you will see a purchase agreement with our offer for this land. If you would like to move forward with the offer, you can email us a copy of the signed purchase agreement to **(Your email)** or mail in the signed purchase agreement to **(Your address) (Your City), (Your State) (Your Zip).**

If you have any questions at all or would like to discuss the process, please give us a call at **(Your number).**

If you have any other property you are interested in selling, please contact me to discuss further.

Sincerely,

(your name)

(your Email)   **(your phone)**   **(your website)**

(your company)
(your address)
(your city), (your state) (your zip)

Reference #: (Reference)

Sales Contract to Purchase Real Estate

This offer is for the purchase of real estate in **(County) County, (Situs St)**. The purchase price of **(Offer Price)** will be paid in full at the time of closing.

The real estate we are offering to purchase is **(Lot acreage)** acres and its parcel number is **(APN Formatted)**

This offer is contingent upon the following terms:

1. Buyer's confirmation and acceptance of legal and physical aspects of the property
2. This offer shall remain open until **(Closing Date)** and if not accepted by then, the offer shall be rescinded, unless otherwise discussed.
3. Buyer can Take title in any entity of their choosing
4. Buyer will pay for all closing costs

(Your Company)   **Seller**

Buyer Sign: _____   **Owner Name:** _____

                                                   Owner Signature: _____

                                                   Address: _____

                                                   _____

                                                   Phone: _____

                                                   Email: _____

(your Email)   **(your phone)**   **(your website)**

Sales Agreement

County, State:
APN:
Acreage:
Legal Description: **"As Seen on deed"**

The purchase price of _____ will be paid in full at the time of closing unless otherwise discussed. The buyer will pay for the costs of completing the transaction.

This offer is contingent upon the following terms:
1. Buyer is to put down a deposit of $499.00 to hold the property, held by _____. This deposit will go towards the purchase of the property
2. If the buyer is unable to provide funds at closing, the buyer will lose the $499.00 down payment unless otherwise discussed.
3. Buyer will be refunded deposit if it does not clear title and is not insurable
4. Closing will occur on or before _____

Company Name (Seller)   (Buyer)

Seller (Sign) _____
                              Buyer 1 Name (Print): _____

Seller (Print) _____
                              Buyer 1 (sign): _____

                              Buyer 2 Name (Print): _____

                              Buyer 2 (Sign): _____

                              Current Address: _____

                              _____

                              Phone:_____

                              Email:_____

Company Name LLC   **901-111-1111**   **Support@companyname.com**

ACKNOWLEDGMENTS

Writing this book has been an incredible journey, and I couldn't have done it without the support of many individuals.

First, I want to express my deepest gratitude to my mom, Ellen Apke, and my dad, John Apke. Thank you both for your unwavering support and love, and for helping me become the person I am today and continue to strive to be.

To my brother and business partner, Ron Apke, thank you for being on this journey with me. Your partnership, friendship, and dedication have been crucial to building our vision together.

I am also grateful to the incredible team at Land Investing Online and The Land Portal. Your hard work and commitment to excellence have helped bring our shared goals to life.

To everyone who believed in this project, from editors to early readers—your insights and support have been invaluable in making this book what it is.

Finally, to you, the reader: thank you for taking the time to invest in your financial future. I hope this book serves as a guide and inspiration as you embark on your journey to financial freedom, *one lot at a time.*

ABOUT THE AUTHOR

Daniel Apke is an American serial entrepreneur, real estate and land investor, e-commerce marketing professional, educator, and podcast host. He is the CEO and Co-Founder of Apke Land and Land Investing Online.

Apke graduated from Ohio University with a B.A. in Business Management: Strategic Leadership and Management. Daniel bought his first rental property in 2017 and has added many more properties to his rental portfolio since then. In 2020, Daniel and his brother, Ron Apke, established Apke Land, a firm that specializes in buying and selling vacant land across several states in the United States. Daniel currently serves as the Chief Executive Officer of the company. One year later, Daniel co-founded Land Investing Online, an educational platform that aims at educating people on how to start and run a profitable land flipping business.

Along with his brother Ron, Daniel also hosts a podcast named "The Real Estate Investing Podcast." He also owns a drop-shipping, a blog, and a YouTube channel, where he shares his knowledge, experience, opinions, and information about online businesses, investment, and real estate topics. He has been featured in several leading publications and magazines including *Yahoo Finance, Seeking Alpha, The Wall Street Journal, Finanzen.net, Morning Star, and Benzinga.*